building great
SCHOOL BOARD–
SUPERINTENDENT
teams

A Systematic
Approach to
Balancing
Roles and
Responsibilities

Bradley V. Balch
Michael T. Adamson

Solution Tree | Press

a division of
Solution Tree

555 North Morton Street
Bloomington, IN 47404
800.733.6786 (toll free) / 812.336.7700
FAX: 812.336.7790

email: info@SolutionTree.com
SolutionTree.com

Visit **go.SolutionTree.com/leadership** to download the free reproducibles in this book.

Printed in the United States of America

21   20   19   18   17   1   2   3   4   5

Library of Congress Cataloging-in-Publication Data

Names: Balch, Bradley V., author. | Adamson, Michael T., author.

Title: Building great school board-superintendent teams : a systematic

    approach to balancing roles and responsibilities / Bradley V. Balch,

    Michael T. Adamson.

Description: Bloomington, IN : Solution Tree Press, [2018] | Includes

    bibliographical references and index.

Identifiers: LCCN 2017015362 | ISBN 9781945349133 (perfect bound)

Subjects: LCSH: School board-superintendent relationships.

Classification: LCC LB2831 .B34 2018 | DDC 379.1/531--dc23 LC record available at https://lccn.loc.
gov/2017015362

Solution Tree
Jeffrey C. Jones, CEO
Edmund M. Ackerman, President

Solution Tree Press
President and Publisher: Douglas M. Rife
Editorial Director: Sarah Payne-Mills
Managing Production Editor: Caroline Cascio
Production Editor: Alissa Voss
Senior Editor: Amy Rubenstein
Copy Editor: Ashante K. Thomas
Cover and Text Designer: Abigail Bowen
Editorial Assistants: Jessi Finn and Kendra Slayton

[acknowledgments]

I would like to thank my wife, Tonya, for her unyielding support and encouragement throughout the development of this book. Tonya exemplifies the concept of "team!"

—**Brad Balch**

First, I am most thankful for the blessing that is my wife, Ella; she undoubtedly has been and continues to be my greatest supporter. Second, I want to thank Dr. Balch for honoring me with the invitation to collaborate with him in this endeavor—what a great adventure this has been! Last, but certainly not least, to superintendents and school board members—although the good work you do and the selfless contributions of knowledge, experience, and time may often go unnoticed by the people you represent, allow me to say "thank you" for steadfastly representing your districts' best interests in public education leadership and governance oversight.

—**Michael Adamson**

Solution Tree Press would like to thank the following reviewers:

Howard Carlson
Superintendent
Wickenburg Unified School District 9
Wickenburg, Arizona

Suzanne Darmer
Former Superintendent
Ada Exempted Village School District
Ada, Ohio

William Crandall
Superintendent
Lake Superior School District
Two Harbors, Minnesota

Lois DaSilva-Knapton
Superintendent
Canterbury Public Schools
Canterbury, Connecticut

Debra Pace
Superintendent
School District of Osceola County
Kissimmee, Florida

Kelly Pew
Superintendent
Rock Hill School District 3
Rock Hill, South Carolina

Flora Reichanadter
Superintendent
Metropolitan School District of Pike
  Township
Indianapolis, Indiana

Brian Schmitt
Superintendent
Genesee Valley School District
Belmont, New York

Nikolai Vitti
Superintendent
Duval County Public Schools
Jacksonville, Florida

Martin Waters
Superintendent
Evans County Schools
Claxton, Georgia

Visit **go.SolutionTree.com/leadership** to download the free reproducibles in this book.

[table of contents]

[part i]

Chapter 3
Team Members' Roles and Responsibilities 35

Chapter 4
Effective Communication and a Unified Voice 45

Chapter 5
Team Decision Making 59

Chapter 6
Committed and Effective Team Leadership 71

[part ii]

Chapter 11
System Evaluation Essentials 137

Chapter 12
The Future of the School Board–
Superintendent Team 149

References and Resources 155

Index 161

[about the authors]

 **Bradley V. Balch, PhD,** is a professor and dean emeritus at Indiana State University. He is a graduate faculty member in the department of educational leadership at Bayh College of Education, and an affiliate faculty member in the department of management, information systems, and business education at Scott College of Business. Balch has been a former superintendent, principal, assistant principal, and teacher throughout West Central Indiana. Balch was also a two-term board member and president for the Covington Community School Corporation in Covington, Indiana. He has been an educator of industrial technology and mathematics since 1984, having taught kindergarten through twelfth grade in a variety of school settings. His educational experiences range from working in rural settings to urban schools with a range of socioeconomic statuses and academic performances, including the North Montgomery School Corporation in Crawfordsville, Indiana, and the Vigo County School Corporation in Terre Haute, Indiana.

Balch served on the board of directors for the American Association of Colleges for Teacher Education from 2012 to 2015. He also served on the board of directors for the Teacher Education Council of State Colleges and Universities from 2008 through 2016 and was president from 2011 through 2012. Balch is a member of the Indiana Association of School Principals and, in 2012, won its President's Award. Balch strongly believes in continuous school improvement and the power of strong leadership and governance at the district level to restore trust and confidence in local control. He has given more than 140 presentations throughout the United States and internationally, on topics ranging from accreditation and continuous improvement to leadership and governance imperatives. Balch has authored or coauthored more than fifty publications, including two books, *Transformational Leadership and Decision Making in Schools* and *Preparing a Professional Portfolio: A School Administrator's Guide*.

Balch received a bachelor of science degree in education from Ball State University, a master of arts in education from Ball State University, and a doctorate of philosophy in educational administration from Indiana State University.

To learn more about Bradley V. Balch' s work, follow @BalchBrad on Twitter.

 **Michael T. Adamson, EdD,** is the director of board services at the Indiana School Boards Association (ISBA), a position he has held since 2006 after retiring from his thirty-one-year tenure as a purchasing program manager at General Motors. Adamson is also a former school board member of the Avon Community School Corporation in Avon, Indiana, having served for twenty years.

Adamson is a member of the National Affiliation of Superintendent Searchers through the National School Boards Association and has been primarily responsible for the oversight and facilitation of professional development activities for school board members throughout Indiana as director of board services. He has also served as a resource for the Indiana Association of Public School Superintendents for training in superintendent evaluation preparation and has written for the magazine *School Administrator*. He has also presented for the Indiana Association of School Business Officials Leadership Academy on school board–administrator relationships. In addition to his presentations and facilitation support for Indiana's 289 traditional K–12 public school districts, Adamson also serves as the editor and contributing writer to the ISBA's quarterly magazine, *The Journal*.

Adamson received a bachelor of science degree in business administration, a master of science in management, a master of arts in leadership studies, and a doctorate of education degree in organizational leadership from Indiana Wesleyan University.

To book Bradley V. Balch or Michael T. Adamson for professional development, contact pd@SolutionTree.com.

Introduction

> It must be considered that there is nothing more difficult to carry out, nor more doubtful of success, nor more dangerous to handle, than to initiate a new order of things.
> **—Niccolò Machiavelli**

The 21st century's change-fraught education environment has large and looming implications for local school boards and superintendents. A sense of urgency is surging around teaching and learning, with all types of education stakeholders demanding, or at least expecting, continuous improvement, ample alternatives, and quick solutions to persistent challenges such as poverty's fallout and limited resources. How are local school boards and superintendents to react to such persistent challenges, especially when immersed in such urgency? John Kotter (2008), a best-selling author and authority on leadership and change, notes, "Urgency is a combination of thoughts, feelings, and actual behavior." In part, this book aims to address the thoughts, feelings, and behaviors needed for school boards and superintendents to function effectively as a team in an environment demanding quick and sustained improvement. Additionally, John Mannes (2015) believes, "Our national conversation on education should include more discussion of effective school system leadership" (p. 23). We hope this book contributes much to that broader conversation as well.

One of this book's main foci is ensuring that each school board–superintendent team provides effective leadership through a deep understanding of each member's role and responsibilities. Much difficulty stems from the considerable position overlap of a school board member and a superintendent. Consider the following list of desirable skills for both a superintendent and a school board member in a local newspaper (see figure I.1, page 2). Many roles and responsibilities for both positions are similar and require common attributes.

The school board member and superintendent must both be able to:

- **Lead** a complex educational organization
- **Affirm** mission, vision, and core values
- **Create** or **support** viable policy
- **Allocate** human and fiscal resources wisely
- **Handle** conflict via negotiations, compromise, and human relations practices
- **Build** new and more substantive school-community relations
- **Support** major school improvement efforts
- **Provide** adequate facilities
- **Tolerate** ambiguity and uncontrollable events
- **Respect** student, faculty, and parent rights

- **Understand** diversity issues and effectively **collaborate** with interest groups and coalitions
- **Do** what is necessary with poorly performing employees
- **Help** capable employees become even better
- **Demonstrate** ability to work with teachers' unions and other coalitions
- **Support** curriculum that is aligned with state standards
- **Ensure** all students learn
- **Encourage** grants and other creative funding resources
- **Be willing** to work as needed
- **Advocate** for safe school initiatives

Figure I.1: Superintendent and school board member desirable skills.

While the list illustrates the common leadership skills required from both the superintendent and school board member, it also highlights the many demands these same leaders face. School boards and superintendents who address these representative demands together, as opposed to working discretely, greatly improve their odds of successfully working in the complex environment of board governance and district-level leadership. Simply stated, school boards and superintendents will function more effectively as district leaders if they work as a team with common goals, instead of as individual entities.

Local school boards and superintendents must pay close attention to the challenging forces bearing down on school districts or risk losing the citizenry's confidence in their capacity to improve education. A clear understanding of their roles and responsibilities and a commitment to thinking and acting strategically will help these individuals counter the pressures and urgency surrounding school district leadership. If local school boards and superintendents are not prepared to lift the mantle of change and to do so in short order, confidence will shift from the local level to state and national levels as the most equipped to successfully address educational challenges. And while Michael Kirst and Frederick Wirt (2009) anticipate the "future boards' role will remain intact and similar to the past" (p. 154), they also share the belief that local control may give way to increased involvement from higher levels of government. If public confidence is to migrate back to the local level in the future, it is imperative that boards and superintendents function effectively as a team.

Although this book emphasizes the notion of a team, we acknowledge the differences in the school board and superintendent roles and do not recommend that districts force a degree of teamwork that would negate these unique responsibilities. The superintendent's role is one of chief executive officer (CEO), and an elected or appointed school board evaluates and hires him or her. The superintendent generally informs the board's business, which it accomplishes at public meetings. The superintendent has a voice during these public meetings but does not vote. These differences delineate roles and responsibilities, and in some cases, such as with evaluation, it would be unwise to force role and responsibility overlap. We acknowledge differences such as this throughout the book as appropriate, but most content is dedicated to the areas where team potential exists.

The Power of a Team Approach

The relationship between and role of school boards and superintendents has changed over time, accompanying changes in each entity's role and governing style. However, for the most part, boards and superintendents functioned independently of each other, with the result being a quasi-corporate model in which the superintendent was the educational expert charged with ensuring student success and the board governed the district with a responsibility to its electorate. Before 1900, superintendents served as general supervisors to their schools while board members served as the administrative body, attending to things such as coal purchasing to heat the school. From 1900 through the 1930s, superintendents assumed a more executive role and school boards a corporate-style model of governance. By the 1940s, superintendents had become professional educators and school boards set general policy (Tyack & Hansot, 1982), a trend that continued throughout the 20th century (Carter & Cunningham, 1997). As of 2000, boards and superintendents seem to work as a partnership (Glass, Björk, & Brunner, 2000). Over time, superintendents and school boards have increasingly shared responsibility for what were distinct roles—ensuring student success and serving an electorate (education stakeholders and community patrons) in a political environment.

Drastic changes in the number of individuals associated with these positions accompanied the changes in the superintendent's and school board's role. Although consolidation began around 1900, there were still over 195,000 school districts in 1917 (Kirst & Wirt, 2009). Districts have experienced continually declining numbers since then, and as of 2017, only slightly over 13,800 districts remain, consisting of approximately 90,000 local school board members (National School Boards Association [NSBA], n.d.). While the rate of consolidation has slowed, a 93 percent decline since 1917 has clearly impacted the nature of the school board and superintendent relationship. School boards and superintendents now serve much larger regions, represent far more constituents, and serve a much larger student population than was the case in 1917. These changes, in addition to 21st century educational reforms (such as high-stakes testing, rigorous academic standards, heightened teacher accountability, achievement gaps around poverty and majority or minority status, and international comparisons) and the negative narrative surrounding education, constitute a challenging environment for most boards and superintendents.

To successfully navigate these demands, the 21st century school board and superintendent relationship must be underscored by a unique partnership that acknowledges role and responsibility overlap. That overlap may create tension between the school board and superintendent; however, this tension is manageable. In this book, we emphasize the *team*. The school board–superintendent team is a leadership and governance imperative if we want to restore trust and confidence in local control for education—the key purpose of this book.

School boards' and superintendents' meaningful voice, strangely, seems largely absent in reform efforts—save for the expectation that they direct resources to support building-level administrators, teachers, and staff. Rather, education reform efforts to date largely focus on the school site. Yet, amidst that emphasis, we maintain no one is better positioned to offer a systems-level perspective on issues of school reform than school boards and superintendents.

We believe the school board and superintendents are key in seeing that everything in the district connects to everything else, and that these connections provide the impetus for sustainable improvement. However, a team effort best supports an effective systems-level view. Without a team approach, school districts may encounter a leadership group in which decisions are made hastily in an environment where some individuals have background information and others do not. Board–superintendent teamwork minimizes the divide-and-conquer dangers of working individually and strengthens both entities. It also improves the status of the team in the eyes of education stakeholders both internal and external to the district. Both benefits reinforce the fact that solo leadership rarely trumps team efforts. Working as a team translates to a more powerful governance and leadership presence, something that is clearly needed in 21st century school districts.

The Need for Systematic Implementation

Anyone who has worked toward personal or professional improvement understands the benefits of implementing a change systematically. For example, if the board–superintendent team prioritizes districtwide continuous improvement, it might consider several steps part of a systematic approach. The team can accomplish some steps, such as vision and mission statement development, more easily than the detail-oriented work of transforming data into useful information. However, the difficulty of creating useful information does not relieve the team from the responsibility of completing this step. Picking select continuous-improvement steps while disregarding others will not yield comprehensive continuous improvement that the team so desires.

Thus, this book intends to provide superintendents, school board members, and school administrators with a systematic approach to building an effective school board–superintendent team. While the recommendations in some chapters are easier to accomplish than others, it is impossible to form an effective leadership and governance team while disregarding some chapters. If a team is further along on some effectiveness measures than others, we recommend using these chapters to affirm its ongoing teamwork before continuing on with the remaining chapters. The following provides brief chapter outlines of the book's two parts.

The first part of the book discusses legal perspectives and teamwork and leadership strategies that should be employed on an ongoing basis to ensure a successful school board–superintendent team. In chapter 1, we examine the importance of effective school governance through a legal lens, including the power and authority afforded a basic governmental unit and how the team can effectively utilize this latitude. Chapter 2 offers strategies for new team member induction and orientation in detail. It describes best practice concepts, with rich implementation ideas for the team. Chapter 3 clarifies who does what and helps teams negotiate the delicate balance of roles and responsibilities to maximize predictability and effectiveness in day-to-day work. The means to communicate effectively as a team is chapter 4's focus, with an emphasis on valuing divergent views and inviting difference to inform a one-voice perspective. Chapter 5 details the step-by-step process leading to informed decision making, whether mundane daily decisions or difficult high-profile decisions. In chapter 6, we focus on providing affirmation opportunities for strong teams and reorientation for weaker teams. We describe a thoughtful process, understanding that team effectiveness and commitment take time and are not achieved in a day or two.

In the second part of the book, we discuss a team approach to the strategic and evaluative functions of school district leadership. We begin in chapter 7 to develop a deeper understanding of how to create core values and beliefs, mission, and vision statements and to understand their important role in guiding the team's governance for the district. Chapter 8 details a systems approach to strategic planning and continuous improvement. It describes multiple models, acknowledging there is no one-size-fits-all model. Chapter 9 addresses the key elements of approaching change agendas, systematic ways of dealing with change, and the means to create a culture that supports openness to change. Chapter 10 deals with strategies to build the board's collective capacity for negating the behavior of rogue members, as well as the means to minimize bad behavior when it occurs. Then, chapter 11 discusses elements of effective evaluation, with strategies to appraise, analyze, and reflect on the aggregated evaluation data. We discuss multiple types of stakeholder feedback to inform team evaluation. Finally, chapter 12 summarizes the book's main ideas and discusses the future of the school board–superintendent team. Each chapter also includes a professional development activity to help teams instill the concepts each chapter covers and to improve their ability to work together, which we discuss next. Visit **go.SolutionTree.com/leadership** to access free reproducible versions of these activities.

The Importance of Professional Development

Effective school board–superintendent teams pursue professional development regularly. Chuck Dervarics and Eileen O'Brien (2011) evidence professional development as a top effectiveness characteristic when they state, "Effective school boards take part in team development and training, sometimes with their superintendents, to build shared knowledge, values and commitments for their improvement efforts." We also recognize the value of professional development, especially when approached as a school board–superintendent team. In each of the twelve chapters, we have developed specific professional development activities that contextualize the chapter content in a way that recognizes and values the many board–superintendent team differences that undoubtedly exist. These team-building activities are found directly after the relevant chapter text that they support—some activities are at the end of the chapter and some appear throughout the chapter, depending on the content. The activities should add value and meaning to each chapter topic given the unique contexts of each school board–superintendent team, while strengthening overall team effectiveness.

Professional development, as presented in this book, strengthens team relationships, improves congeniality and collegiality, deepens trust and respect among team members, and enhances individual members' general habits of mind related to team effectiveness. Teams must allow for vulnerability to maximize the activities' benefits. Vulnerability is too often associated with negative emotions people like to avoid, such as weakness, fear, loss of control, and unhappiness. In efforts to be invulnerable, we often avoid or suppress discussions that reveal our imperfections, shortcomings, lack of knowledge, and feelings in general. However, avoiding vulnerability has the negative effect of communicating that we are not authentic, truthful, trusting, or approachable. Great strength lies in vulnerability. The willingness to participate fully in the activities shared in this book builds individual and team trust, encourages truthful disclosure, places a high value on differences, promotes an openness to risk, and strengthens the professional relationship among team members necessary to function effectively. These benefits are difficult to derive in the absence of a willingness to be vulnerable.

Professional Development Activity on Teamwork

This introductory professional development activity helps team members practice engaging as a team for meaningful growth. The activity builds on the rationale that effective boards pursue professional development and that vulnerability is necessary for optimal teamwork.

Time Frame

The team needs approximately fifteen to thirty minutes to complete the activity.

Materials

The team needs a facilitator and the quotable quotes contained in figure I.2 (page 8). Figure I.2 should be distributed to each member or displayed publicly.

Process

The superintendent or one board member should volunteer to serve as a facilitator. The facilitator should:

1. Ask team members to view the list of quotes in figure I.2 (page 8) and ponder the following question: "As you think about the school board and superintendent as a team, which quote best describes the team from your perspective and why?" Please note that if team members have a quote they would prefer to use instead, they may do so.

- "Nothing ventured, nothing gained."
- "Go for the gusto."
- "Activity doesn't mean productivity."
- "Ready, fire, aim."
- "Time waits for no one."
- "Slow but sure."
- "Look before you leap."
- "Opportunity knocks but once."
- "Seize the day."
- "When in Rome, do as the Romans do."
- "All things are possible once it is realized that everything is at stake."
- "Success is not a doorway; it's a staircase."
- "When you're on thin ice, you might as well dance."

Figure I.2: Quotable quotes.

*Visit **go.SolutionTree.com/leadership** to download a free reproducible version of this figure.*

2. Ask each team member to volunteer his or her answer and rationale. (Other team members may ask questions for clarity, but no answer should be judged.)

3. Restate the common areas of strength, challenge, or both that team members shared and how this information might help the team in the future.

Results

Participating in this activity strengthens trust among the team, encourages truthful disclosure, emphasizes team members' differences, and contributes to stronger relationships, which builds a more effective team.

Summary

Local school boards and superintendents must provide leadership and governance in a challenging environment, one that is characterized by the need for continuous improvement, ample alternatives, and quick solutions to persistent challenges. A strong sense of urgency, or even crisis in some cases, further amplifies these challenges. Over time, patrons have increasingly lost confidence in local control as the catalyst for meaningful change, instead preferring direct intervention from state and federal sources to solve difficult education woes.

If local school boards and superintendents are to restore confidence in the local school district leadership and governance ability, they must adapt to the practice of functioning as a school board–superintendent team. This team must embrace the idea that some level of role and responsibility overlap will occur, and must be comfortable with the predictable tension that manifests from role and responsibility overlap. This book aims to make the case for a school board–superintendent team and provide the necessary cornerstones for the team to function effectively. It is equally hoped this book will support aspiring school board members and preservice superintendents to build the requisite skills needed for success prior to serving on the team.

part i

Teamwork and
Leadership
Strategies for
School Board–
Superintendent
Teams

Chapter 1

Legal Perspectives and the Case for Local Control

For school boards and district administrators to operate effectively, school board–superintendent team members must understand and embrace the parameters of their governing power. While states and provinces vary on the extent power and control of day-to-day educational operations are delegated to the local level, one thing is consistent: boards form the basic governmental unit, functioning as an agency to deliver the states' or provinces' promise of a free public education. Superintendents serve as the legal administrator, duly empowered by board approval. The school board–superintendent team finds precedents of civil and common law in constitutions, case law, state or provincial law, and federal law, and administrative codes circumscribe its overall conduct. Though national and state or provincial laws set the guidelines, their execution is locally administered.

At a period of time in education when control at the local level feels minimal and education stakeholders expect and demand broad latitude regarding choice and expression, governing powers related to teaching and learning are actually broad in scope if utilized effectively and fully understood. For many board–superintendent teams, a *home rule* concept applies, in which the team is able to exercise great latitude over educational operations doing everything necessary for the district unless legally prohibited in doing so (Wolf & Bolinder, 2009). This chapter builds a rational basis for renewed enthusiasm related to local control in which board–superintendent teams have much control over teaching and learning in their districts. Given the broad array of legal examples that could be considered in a chapter such as this, dress codes will be used as the basis for examples and professional development, as this is an issue all boards must deal with and a genuine test of team effectiveness.

Educational Governance and the U.S. Constitution

The U.S. founders were very intentional in not mentioning *education* when developing the country's Constitution. There was recognition among the founders of the need for the sovereignty of the states as commonwealths, and a strong commitment to a federal system (diffusion of governing power from the federal to the state level, with a localized emphasis) as opposed to a national system (centralized governing power at the federal level). There was also much fear among the founders that a nationalized system would lead to a single educational doctrine, something they intentionally wanted to avoid. As a federal, not national, system, the United States is organized as a union of states with a central government; however, by virtue of the U.S. Constitution's Tenth Amendment, systems of public education are delegated to the states (Alexander & Alexander, 2012).

Understanding the team's basic sources of governing power can shed insight into the broad governing powers afforded to the team, ultimately enhancing overall effectiveness. The following list illustrates a representative pathway from the U.S. Constitution to a basic governmental unit.

- **U.S. Constitution:** This document does not contain the word *education*, an intentional omission to support a federalized (meaning localized) educational system.

- **Tenth Amendment to the U.S. Constitution:** This amendment is the basis for delegating education to the states.

- **Fourteenth Amendment to the U.S. Constitution:** This complicated amendment ensures no person is denied life, liberty, or property rights without due process. Educational rights are considered property rights (Board of Regents of State Colleges v. Roth, 1972).

- **State constitutions:** Each state constitution has provisions for a free public education and delegates authority to its state legislatures to develop a system of education (Schimmel, Stellman, & Fischer, 2014).

- **State statutes:** Each state statute is an expression of legislative will and state law, and the means by which schools are governed since school districts have no inherent powers. State statutes express or imply school district powers (Alexander & Alexander, 2012).

- **Federal and state case law:** These refer to court interpretations of law based on statutes that originated from the legislative bodies. These interpretations are also known as common law (Alexander & Alexander, 2012).

- **Other sources of school law:** These sources might include the following—
  - Rules from state and federal administrative agencies
  - Master contracts
  - Board policy or guidelines

It is clear that the founders of the United States intended for school district governance to be conducted at the local level; thus, board–superintendent teams must build confidence in their governing ability and abide by state and local legislation when governing. It is also crucial for governing teams to strive for balance between the competing priorities of commonwealth and sovereignty, as we discuss in the following section.

Commonwealth and Sovereignty Principles

As with most governance, issues related to people and agencies can be competing, such that ground may be gained in one area only for another area to lose ground. These issues often involve the competing priorities of commonwealth and sovereignty. A federalized system is built on the notion of a *commonwealth*, in which a collection of people enjoins as part of a state. In fact, due to this definition, the terms *state* and *commonwealth* are often used interchangeably. The state enjoys sovereign powers, meaning there should be no power over the state to influence decisions. As mentioned earlier, the state's citizens enjoy life, liberty, and property rights, which include the right to an education (Board of Regents of State Colleges v. Roth, 1972). The competing dimension of these powerful freedoms comes with the idea that being part of a sovereign state also means being part of a commonwealth. To enjoy the advantages of being a part of something larger than ourselves (for instance, a commonwealth with sovereign powers), we must be willing to give up some individual rights for the commonwealth's good. Similarly, in education, many stakeholders (such as students, parents, faculty, staff, and administrators) give up some individual freedoms to be part of a larger educational system and receive the benefits of a public education.

To illustrate this exchange of freedoms, we will consider the example of dress codes. As individuals, we have the right to free expression vis-à-vis how we dress. An individual can wear something controversial and roam the streets of a community exercising his or her freedom of expression, even if others are offended or disagree. In a school setting, however, these same individual rights of expression can be limited and restricted if tied to valid educational purposes. For example, the board–superintendent team may consider certain clothing colors, patterns, or logos to be gang-related or prone to creating conflicts in the school setting, which may disrupt teaching and learning. As a result, these clothing items may subsequently be prohibited in school grounds or at school-related events to avoid disrupting education—a limitation of individual freedoms for the common good of all students receiving a public education. Ultimately, it is the board–superintendent team that considers community norms, its educational purposes, and attendant dress restrictions necessary for quality teaching and learning to occur in the district. This is just one of many strategic decisions a board–superintendent team must consider in which individual rights are limited for all to enjoy an education.

Professional Development Activity on Power and Control

This activity helps team members practice utilizing the appropriate levels of power and control afforded a school board–superintendent team. It builds on the rationale that school board–superintendent teams function as a basic governmental unit and that, in the spirit of sovereignty, teams will often have to make difficult decisions that limit individual freedoms to advance the district's educational purposes. Teams will practice making a difficult decision relating to a topic most board–superintendent teams will deal with: dress codes. They will also learn how to justify the reasoning behind that decision and the use of that power to external stakeholders.

Time Frame

The team should allow approximately sixty minutes for this activity.

Materials

This activity requires a facilitator, a computer with Internet access, and a projector.

Process

The facilitator should take the following steps.

1. Access a video clip on a dress code case involving a local school board. Consider "Washington School District May Change Dress Code" (WTAE-TV Pittsburgh, 2012; www.goo.gl/fEVioC) or "Some Schools Tighten Dress Codes" (KOAT New Mexico, 2012; www.goo.gl/h4N6bv). Please note that video links often change or are removed. If these are no longer available, the facilitator can search the key words *dress code* and *local school board* to reveal other options.

2. Consider what led to the controversy in the video and select a controversial aspect of the district's dress code for discussion.

3. Ask each team member to prove that the aspect of the dress code being considered "materially disrupts classwork or involves substantial disorder or invasion of the rights of others" (Tinker v. Des Moines Independent Community School District, 1969). The following clarifying questions may help.

    - "Can you show discipline is greater at school in the absence of the dress code restriction or that the dress code restriction has reduced discipline?"

    - "Was the teacher disrupted, unable to teach or both?"

    - "Was student learning disrupted?"

    - "Was there so much discussion about the dress code topic among students that the teacher had difficulty starting or continuing class?

    - "Did disruptions such as fighting, bullying, harrassment, or threats occur because of the dress code?"

4. Explain that dress restrictions put in place to prevent something such as gang activity need to show evidence of a connection. The school or district can also "take reasonable action to restrict student expression" (Schimmel et al., 2014, p. 164) before an actual disruption occurs if there is a "reasonable likelihood of substantial disorder" (Karp v. Becken, 1973). The facilitator should ask, "If applicable, are you able to evidence this?"

5. Regarding emblem and symbol restrictions, does it "convey a particularized message . . . [that] would be understood by those who viewed it" (Olesen v. Board of Education, 1987)? For example, would a particular type of jewelry or a symbol such as a unique image of a certain color communicate gang involvement and would others interpret it as gang involvement? If so, then the restriction would be appropriate. If the symbol or image does not communicate something disruptive or contrary to educational purposes and is not viewed as disruptive and contrary to educational purposes by others, then what is the reason for the restriction?

6. Point out that districts or schools must be careful of gender discrimination. Have the team consider, "Does the aspect selected for discussion differentiate between males and females? If so, why does one gender have a heavier dress code burden than the other?" In other words, can each team member prove a legitimate, nondiscriminatory reason for the dress code restriction that has a "reasonable relationship" to education in the school or district (Johnson v. Joint School District No. 60, 1973)?

7. Confer with the team whether the aspect of the dress code selected for discussion truly supports social norms in the district's community. While many districts have dress code restrictions they believe support community norms, it may be that the team's community supports tolerance and diversity, which would allow for dress code minimums, not restrictions.

8. Close by discussing next-step actions as a result of the activity. How could the team prevent the same controversy from happening in their own district? Should other dress code issues be discussed in a similar manner? Should current dress codes be delegated back to the school levels for review? Finally, how did this activity raise the team's awareness of limiting individual rights to advance educational purposes?

Results

Participating in this activity supports the impact of a basic governmental unit (the board–superintendent team), highlighting that this particular team wields considerable power and control. Effectively using this power and control enhances team functioning.

This power can be intimidating and challenging for team members. The preceding considerations for dress code restrictions are only a representative example of the questions the board–superintendent team should be asking itself. Further, this is only one topic among many that may require a prudent legal lens to ensure educational appropriateness. Sound legal counsel can prove most helpful when considering such topics as dress codes.

Governance Within the School Board–Superintendent Team

Given the historical context of school board–superintendent teams and the legal perspectives that empower a local locus of control, we now turn our attention to the legalities of governing within the team. School board–superintendent teams must adhere to certain legal requirements in their actions and must be able to justify their decisions in a legal setting, if necessary. We will discuss two of these issues in the following sections: (1) operating under basic democratic principles and (2) meeting expectations for legal scrutiny.

Operating Under Basic Democratic Principles

Governmental units, such as school districts, are compelled to operate under basic democratic principles. In its simplest form, governing democratically is governing "by the people for the people" (Lincoln, 1863). As elected and appointed officials, school board members represent interests much larger than any one person. They are the voice of all the people they serve. The same principle is true for the superintendent, who is duly appointed as the chief executive officer and is assumed to be the most highly trained professional among all educators in the district. The superintendent's professional ethics dictate "exemplary professional conduct . . . recognizing that his or her actions will be viewed and appraised by the community, professional associates, and students" (American Association of School Administrators [AASA], n.d.). The old adage "all politics are local" takes on new meaning for both school board members and superintendents as they make the effort to appropriately represent all key stakeholders in the communities they serve.

An expanded interpretation of governing democratically means that everyone on the board–superintendent team may present a point of view and that all sides must be heard and considered. More important, the team must place value on all points of view before making a decision. Those individuals opposing the will of the majority should be open to a decision contrary to theirs and committed to supporting this will publicly, as well (see also One Unified Voice, page 52). School board–superintendent teams should consider whether all voices are valued among their team members. Is there a unified front of support after a final decision is made? If not, the board–superintendent team should consider why this is the case and work toward a level of openness in which every voice is valued, even when there is disagreement among opinions on a particular topic. Valuing individual voices is an important measure of effectiveness because it implies the team genuinely considers differences—an important attribute to model in any community.

Meeting Expectations for Legal Scrutiny

Based on centuries of tradition, courts make intentional efforts to not question the judgment of the executive or legislative branches and their respective agencies, including school districts. This is considered part of the government's separation of powers. Additionally, courts usually adhere to the concept of *stare decisis*, or "let the decision stand" ("stare decisis," 2017). Considered wise policy, this concept relies on past court decisions, creating a historical development of legal controversies with fairly predictable outcomes. Further, the lower courts are much more likely to adhere to the decisions of higher courts in the same jurisdiction. In sum, court systems are generally stable, consistent, and predictable in their rulings, expecting school districts are posturing in much the same way. Accordingly, actions among the board–superintendent team must be enacted conscientiously with due deliberation and not in a way that is arbitrary (for example, not based on reason) or capricious (for example, changing often and quickly).

Teams may like to consider the following non-exhaustive list of legal cornerstones for board–superintendent team actions whether facing student- or adult-related issues, to help ensure effective decisions that meet minimal expectations for legal scrutiny.

- **Take time to receive ample input on issues of concern so that an informed decision can be made:** There's a tendency to believe the first version of a story before all information is received (Brower & Balch, 2005). It does require intentional effort to be open to different versions of the truth, and each member on the board–superintendent team should be willing to engage in this level of openness. Receive information as a judge would; have an open mind to diverse perspectives and a willingness to consider multiple points of view.

- **Document, document, document:** Keep a record, whether in the form of private, personal investigative notes, or more official records that could be subject to public review (often the case when notes are shared with others). It is easy to lose track of the details without adequate documentation.

- **Have the board–superintendent team ask (as a minimum) the following questions:**
  - "Is the issue being considered reasonably tied to the district's educational operations?"
  - "What was the educational purpose of our rule or expectation and the subsequent action or actions to deal with the issue?"
  - "Did we act arbitrarily or capriciously so as to restrict individual rights?"
  - "Was our action in the school district's best interests (in order to maintain order and discipline)?"
  - "Does policy or guidelines support our actions?"
  - "Was our action based on valid and defensible reasons?"
  - "Are actions and outcomes disproportionate (excessive or unreasonable) to the issue being considered?"

- **Ensure team members have appropriate discussion and dialogue to clarify questions and concerns:** We all see and hear different things and bring diverse perspectives to an issue. Ample discussion and dialogue ensures that teams make an informed decision.

- **Consider the district's and state school board association's legal counsel perspective before the final decision on an issue:** When considering any or all of these legal cornerstones, teams may decide that best practice would involve seeking assistance from or the opinion of a legal professional. A legal course of action protects the stakeholders in an issue and sets consistent precedent for the team's decisions. The decision to seek legal counsel is wise, and will be discussed in the following section.

Utilizing Legal Counsel

Given the array of business the board–superintendent team must deal with on a monthly basis, it may wish to hire sound legal counsel to help minimize or even negate problems that often emerge from governance when education stakeholders (for example, students, faculty, parents, and vendors) feel wronged. Most board–superintendent teams are conflict averse, focusing instead on building strong relationships with the patrons they serve. This relational focus may be the source of problems if teams attempt to calm, appease, and minimize the problems they are faced with instead of addressing them directly, with the knowledge that conflict, anger, denial, and a host of other uncomfortable emotive outcomes are certain to emerge. These actions may incidentally create due process, policy, or other problems that eventually rise to the level of a legal dispute. In contrast, legal counsel generally focuses on providing clear communications reflecting a sound legal understanding. These two perspectives, while very different, often provide a complementary partnership for board–superintendent teams seeking smooth governance.

We can see the advantage of board–superintendent teams retaining legal counsel by returning again to the example of dress codes. The team should understand free speech rights as a reason to support a less restrictive dress code. For example, a group of vocal parents might approach the board–superintendent team to advocate for a more restrictive dress code based on a rise in T-shirts being worn with an image the group perceives as provocative and controversial. The group's main position is that a dress code restriction better reflects the community's culture. In trying to appease these more visible and vocal patrons who are well respected in the community, the board–superintendent team may consider, codify, and enforce dress code restrictions as a new school-level expectation.

Ultimately, this new rule may lead to a legal challenge from other students and parents on the grounds that it restricts students' rights to freely express themselves. In fact, it may well be that the community's prevailing culture is actually diverse and values differences, but such a culture is overshadowed by a vocal interest group or angry parent at the expense of the broader community. In this case, the initial decision to calm and appease the concerns of one vocal group may lay the groundwork for an indefensible dress code restriction, especially if no sound educational purpose can be proven.

To this point, legal counsel can be most helpful. Legal counsel understands the team's local situational context, current case law, local policy, and guidelines, and can interpret these things to make an informed decision about what might potentially be a disruption or not. District legal counsel's focus on clear communications and sound legal understanding is different than the board–superintendent team's priority focus on building relationships, and while the legal counsel's approach may be a source of tension or strain, a clear communication focus leaves much less room for legal error or erroneous interpretation.

Interestingly, too much focus on either building relationships or sending clear communications with sound legal understanding as a first priority could each challenge the board–superintendent team. Ideally, the board–superintendent team should aim to combine the two qualities—communicating clearly with sound legal understanding while fostering healthy relationships and knowing that a degree of tension may arise along the way. Ultimately, seeking a balance of both priorities while avoiding legal pitfalls is always the objective.

Avoiding Legal Pitfalls

At times, issues of legality may be brought into question to simply avoid a tough discussion. Consider the example of a principal who wishes to put benches in the hallways of her middle school, to make the space more inviting and encourage collaboration. A superintendent who is unwilling to deal with this issue at the time may make the claim, "It's illegal because the fire codes won't let us block the halls with furniture." Further discussion, however, might reveal that furniture in the hallways is legal provided a certain amount of space still exists.

In these situations, legal counsel is useful because their guidance allows creative ideas to come to fruition without being hampered by team members' lack of legal knowledge. Statements like "It's not a bad idea, but it's against regulations" communicate a powerful negative message fraught with distrust, and hamper rather than encourage creativity and collaboration. When someone introduces an idea or suggests a solution to a problem, only to be told "no" because of questions surrounding legal codes, it does not serve to inspire participation, creative thought, or imagination, and it ultimately harms morale and damages relationships. Rather, say, "Tell me more about your idea," or "Help me better understand your solution"—and then turn to the team's legal counsel to clear up any uncertainties. Teams should aim to avoid the decreased trust that comes with stalled discussions while keeping all perspectives informed by the legal question at hand and all discussion within legal parameters.

In sum, the most effective school board–superintendent teams function when they understand the legal parameters defining the scope of their governance. Adopting legal counsel can assist teams in appropriately meeting and communicating their responsibilities to relevant stakeholders and in avoiding legal pitfalls.

Summary

The U.S. founders hoped for a federalized system of education in which no single educational doctrine would prevail. They ensured this, in part, by delegating the power to provide a free public education to the states through the Tenth Amendment and leaving the word *education* absent from the U.S. Constitution (Pulliam & Van Patten, 2003).

As the founders envisioned, states with sovereign powers have broad latitude in developing free public systems of education, and they vary in the degree of power and control they delegate to the most basic governmental unit: the board–superintendent team. States also comprise a commonwealth in which their citizenry forfeits some individual freedoms to enjoy the benefits of state citizenry. Similarly, the principles of a commonwealth impact school districts in that their faculty, staff, administrators, students, and parents all give up something to enjoy the benefits of a public education (Tinker v. Des Moines Independent Community School District, 1969).

Because board–superintendent teams deal with a wide array of issues, sound legal counsel can help minimize or even negate problems that often emerge from governance decision making. The board–superintendent team focus is often different from that of legal counsel. Considering both perspectives can prove most useful when desiring thoughtful, defensible decision making.

Chapter 2

Induction and New Team Member Orientation

Every first-time board member is confronted with the weight of governance as soon as he or she takes the oath of office. Technically, there is no trial period, nor is there an apprenticeship program for aspiring board members. The NSBA (2006) states that a new board member requires the better part of two years before feeling comfortable as a board member. Yet, important decisions requiring the governing body's official vote cannot be delayed until a new member feels comfortable in the role. It is an interesting dilemma, but one that is no different than other roles public officials assume.

Having spoken with numerous school board members over the years, we have discovered the NSBA two-year learning curve claim seems fairly accurate. However, acknowledging that assumption presents another truth, being that a school board's governance effectiveness is potentially compromised anytime a change in its membership dynamic occurs. Expanding on the NSBA's (2006) observation, to operate at peak effectiveness, a school board needs every member to have a minimum of two years' school board experience. This is not an issue for those boards whose membership dynamic changes infrequently, but for school boards that experience membership changes more often—perhaps following election or appointment cycles—the story is very different. For those boards whose memberships frequently change, the logic of the new member learning curve infers that these boards are likely to operate less effectively than boards with less frequent board member turnover.

Do not misunderstand; this deduction does not infer that those boards with higher turnover are incapable of making good decisions or are in a state of dysfunction. Rather, it suggests that it is necessary to quickly indoctrinate new board members in the board's governance culture. Consequently, if there is agreement with the NSBA's two-year learning curve, then an agreement on a method to shorten that cycle is desirable if a school board wishes to achieve maximum effectiveness sooner than two years after seating new members.

The situation is no less disconcerting for the new superintendent. The AASA reports that the average tenure of U.S. superintendents is six years (as cited in Minichello, 2014); therefore, the experience a new superintendent brings to his or her position greatly affects the learning curve cycle. A first-time superintendent does not bring the experience that a more qualified superintendent brings to a new position (Minichello, 2014). Spending time as an administrator at the building level or in central office is helpful for new superintendents, and that experience will serve the novice very well in his or her future dealings with subordinate administrators. However, administrative experience is not the same as the role of a superintendent, nor is the measure of accountability equivalent to the responsibility a school district superintendent shoulders.

Part of the difficulty of hiring a new superintendent equipped with appropriate experience is due to superintendent qualifications varying from state to state (Teacher .org, n.d.):

> A program to become a superintendent will include education classes, administration classes, leadership classes, and developmental classes over the course of many years. A superintendent will also have taken many hours of professional development as a teacher and administrator. . . . Each state can require different qualifications so more information can be gained by researching the area in which you wish to be superintendent.

Consequently, superintendents typically bring a variety of experience to a new position, depending on their individual experiences from various stages and locations in their careers and the skills they have mastered along the way. However, that does not immediately mean that a new superintendent who happens to be a seasoned veteran is more equipped to shoulder the positional responsibilities of a new district any more than a first-time superintendent. What it does mean is that the learning curve will undoubtedly be shorter for the veteran superintendent, depending on the experience that he or she brings to the position.

It is common sense to implement programs for acclimating new school board members to their governing responsibilities, and new superintendents to the practice of balancing management of a multimillion-dollar business and liaisons with governing bodies that oversee public education. New board member–orientation programs are fairly common, and NSBA (2016) encourages them. However, a rigorous orientation agenda is often lacking at the local level when board members first assume their position. This is partly because a lack of common operation protocol exists for school boards and superintendents. In other words, every school board and administration conducts their business a little differently than other school boards and administrations. Each district may function well, but if a board member or the superintendent transferred to a different district, he or she would not immediately be able to function to the same degree of proficiency without some guidance and understanding of the new district's operation and expectation protocol. For this reason, it is imperative to include an introduction to each district's unique functioning style in orientation programs for both board members and superintendents.

There are many reasons to suggest that all school boards and superintendents follow similar operational formats and practices. However, perhaps the greatest reason is to be able to finally remove excuses for ineffectiveness because of the overused mantra, "That's the way *we* do things!" Of course, there is never an excuse for not observing legal statutes or requirements, but those are seldom issues for boards and superintendents from an operational standpoint. Rather, issues more often arise regarding how board members and superintendents function at a professional and interpersonal level in the performance of their distinct, yet complementary, roles.

Although school board associations and superintendent associations offer basic training to new board members and superintendents, this training is typically for an ideal setting and does not consider local practices or idiosyncrasies that deviate from the practices being proposed. This chapter presents a recommended guide to orientation for both new school board members and new superintendents that considers such issues. Although implementing these practices may differ from district to district, common tenets of operation and practice can and should be stressed in any new member orientation program.

Orientation for New School Board Members

An orientation program for new board members that not only familiarizes them with the school district but that also answers some questions about what being a board member in their district means is a basic but essential requirement for every school district. New board members often want answers to the following questions, among others.

- How should the board operate in a public meeting?
- When it is okay to speak?
- What is the protocol for making a motion?
- How does a board member speak to a motion?
- When is discussion permissible?
- What are the ramifications of a non-unanimous vote?
- What is the procedure for bringing an issue before the entire board?

Veteran board members often overlook these basic, but necessary, tenets of board operation when new board members are first seated, but a program tailored to the local district that addresses these basic questions is invaluable for stabilizing the board after seating new members.

A sample school board member orientation program agenda, as seen in figure 2.1, should minimally contain the following items.

---

1. **Personnel overview:** List all administrators, including building administration, staff, and support staff. Include a facilities tour.
2. **School board's role:**
   - Review core values, mission, vision, and strategic plan (goals), and the roles of board members and board officers.
   - Discuss the school board–superintendent relationship. List the superintendent (CEO) and board's (trustee leadership) respective roles in governance. Explain who does what. Include the board-superintendent team expectations.
   - Review meeting protocol, including distribution of support materials (meeting agenda, supporting documents, and inter-meeting updates) and the meeting format.
   - Discuss how to properly engage the public and respond to concerns during and between meetings.
3. **Superintendent's role:** List performance expectations, including annual goals and the evaluation procedure. Outline how the superintendent will evaluate staff and communicate the line of authority.

Figure 2.1: Sample school board member orientation program agenda.
*Visit **go.SolutionTree.com/leadership** to download a free reproducible version of this figure.*

State school board associations cover many of these items in training for new school board members, but what will ultimately resonate with a new member and what is most important is how that training is practically applied at the local level.

If the board does not currently have a new board member orientation program, the preceding outline is a great place to begin, but the board shouldn't forget to personalize the program. The ideal people to help modify the orientation program are the least-senior board members, preferably those in their third or fourth year of their first term of office. They have the most immediate memory of their own new member orientation, and will be most likely to recall what they wished they had known when they were first seated. Incorporate as many items from that list as possible and, rather than having an intensive, one-meeting review, break the session into two or more sessions. This prevents the program from being too overwhelming and fosters opportunities for a constructive question and answer dialogue. Remember, the goal is as much about sharing the established culture and climate of the local board's operation as it is about conveying the mechanics of boardsmanship.

Orientation for New Superintendents

Orientation for new superintendents poses a challenge: his or her responsibilities may differ tremendously from one district to another. In a small district, the superintendent may shoulder all the responsibilities of central office administration, human resources, building maintenance, transportation, chief financial officer, curriculum director, and more. In a large district, the superintendent may primarily oversee other administrators who are responsible for these and other activities. However, regardless of the district's size and the superintendent's role, the one common denominator is that of ultimate responsibility. In other words, if something is wrong, it is the superintendent's fault, and it is the superintendent's responsibility to remedy, whether by direct involvement or by delegation. Superintendents must acknowledge and accept that reality when they assume the position. Such people become superintendents because they desire to occupy that chair, embracing all the responsibility that being *boss* implies.

A practical training program for new superintendents can be a daunting task; however, as with school board members, there are some basic skills that all new superintendents can benefit from.

- Leadership
- School finance
- Effective board–superintendent relations
- Experience with school board members' orientation and training

Leadership

Whether leadership is stressed as part of a licensing curriculum or as part of a program offered through a state superintendent's organization, leadership is a critical piece of the new superintendent's arsenal. Being taught the tenets of leadership does not mean a person is suddenly a leader; it simply means that he or she understands what a leader should be. Plus, understanding what type of leadership is appropriate for a superintendent is vital. Should a superintendent be transformational, transactional, or value-based? Should he or she employ servant leadership, Theory X, or Theory Y (Daft, 2005; O'Toole, 1996)? While it is clear that general leadership skills are important for the superintendent position, more important is what type of leader the superintendent should be.

Leadership training classes are beneficial to identify different leadership styles and to help superintendents understand their own dominant leadership style more completely. Many state superintendent associations, as well as state associations of school business officials, often provide these types of classes in their professional development portfolios. Likewise, state school board associations and private consultants routinely provide workshops and seminars for local school board-superintendent teams to identify and strengthen specific leadership traits within the team.

School Finance

The next basic skill for superintendents is school finance. Understanding school finance is critical for a responsible CEO, whether he or she has direct responsibility for developing the district's budget or whether that responsibility is primarily that of the superintendent's administrative team (assistant superintendents, CFOs, business managers, and so forth). There are multiple avenues to assist new superintendents with acquiring this knowledge: formal classes, other superintendents, the state's Association of School Business Officials, private consultants (often consisting of retired superintendents and retired chief financial officers), and so on. Even if a new superintendent does not have the background and immediate skill set in budget formulation, a reasonable expectation is that he or she will acquire those skills as quickly as possible. That should be the new superintendent's goal as well. If a person is responsible for an organization, it behooves that individual to know as much about everyone else's responsibilities as possible.

The amount of experience superintendents bring to their positions can vary greatly. For instance, superintendents from small districts may be directly responsible for multiple disciplines (such as HR, transportation, budget and finance, and curriculum), while in larger districts, superintendents may have a multi-level administrative teams with individuals who each assume primary responsibility for these specific responsibilities. Consequently, honest conversations with the district superintendent regarding specific training needs are recommended to identify and tailor specific professional development plans and to determine how that can best be accomplished and by whom. Specific resources will vary from state to state but can include colleges, universities, professional organizations such as AASA (The School Superintendents Association), state superintendent associations, state associations of school business officials, and many more.

Effective Board-Superintendent Relations

Next on the list is an understanding of effective board-superintendent relations. This is perhaps the most difficult skill to master, simply because board dynamics have the potential to change dramatically following each election cycle. It is not just a matter of getting along with or befriending board members. Rather, it is about being honest and forthcoming with information and recommendations to illustrate the superintendent's willingness and ability to further the district's vision of education, regardless of popular opinion outside the boardroom or division within the boardroom. Most school board members will readily admit that they do not want a superintendent that simply caters to idle whims and recommendations of the school board. Rather, board members expect educational leadership to provide the best possible public education opportunities possible, and that the superintendent will always act in the best interests of children and taxpayers.

Garnering respect and support not only for the popular recommendations but also for the ones that challenge the status quo for the right reasons is an important leadership characteristic born of personal convictions. As the superintendent develops this skill, he or she will be more likely to receive support from the board when they are asked to donate their limited resources to support a program or initiative, or when he or she asks them to support a district objective that improves the district's ability for increasing student achievement.

Experience With School Board Members' Orientation and Training

A superintendent can also benefit from the orientation and training that school board members receive. By understanding the basic tenets of school governance from a board member's perspective, a superintendent can become better equipped to support and provide his or her board with the appropriate recommendations and support it requires of the district CEO to effectively meet its governance responsibilities.

Understanding the basic requirements of both positions (the school board and superintendent) is the cornerstone that supports all school governance, oversight, and management. However, both school board members and superintendents require *ongoing* professional development that builds on their positions' basic requirements through the exploration and presentation of public education governance thought and practice.

Professional Development Activities for New Team Members

The following activities—Two Truths and a Lie on page 32 and The Truth Seat on page 32—help new members get to know the other team members, and vice versa, to ease the new members' transition. An experienced team may also use the activities to deepen commitment to the team or establish rapport among members. Activities such as these give board members and superintendents a deeper understanding of each other and help them make difficult decisions as team members.

Two Truths and a Lie

This activity encourages team members to share information about themselves and learn things about their team members in a fun and low-pressure environment.

Time Frame
This activity takes fifteen to thirty minutes to complete.

Materials
The team will need a facilitator to encourage responses, pens or pencils for every participant, and notepads.

Process
The facilitator helps the team do the following.

1. Each team member should write down three statements about him- or herself: two truthful statements and one lie.

2. Each person should read his or her three statements aloud in random order. Members should try to state them in the same voice so the lie is not revealed.

3. Once a team member reads the three statements, other team members should guess which one is a lie.

4. The person who shares the statements now clarifies which statement was a lie and explains circumstances about any of the statements made.

5. After everyone has shared their statements, the facilitator summarizes the purpose of the activity and asks for members to share what they have learned about their team members from the activity.

Results
Participation in this activity builds capacity for the team to make difficult decisions by helping team members understand more about each other.

The Truth Seat

This activity promotes honesty and trust through vulnerability.

Time Frame
Teams will need thirty to forty-five minutes to complete this activity.

Materials

The team will need a facilitator to organize the order of team member questioning.

Process

To prepare, the team positions chairs in a half-circle facing a single chair (the *truth seat*). Then, the facilitator supervises the following.

1. Team members take turns sitting in the truth seat until all have had an opportunity.

2. Once a team member is in the truth seat, the other members have a list of questions and may ask the truth seat participant one question. Team members may use the list of questions in figure 2.2, or create their own.

- What has been your greatest professional success or achievement?
- What has been your greatest personal success or achievement?
- What has been your greatest professional disappointment?
- What has been your greatest personal disappointment?
- If you won $1 million, what would you do with it?
- If you could change one thing about education in this country today, what would it be? Why?
- What teacher in your K–12 school experience impacted you most? Why?
- What is the greatest threat facing our school district? Why?
- Who do you believe the most important historical figure in this country's history is? Why?
- What is your favorite, book, movie, or play? Why?

Figure 2.2: The Truth Seat sample questions.

*Visit **go.SolutionTree.com/leadership** to download a free reproducible version of this figure.*

3. The facilitator concludes the activity by discussing points of commonality, any surprising disclosures, what everyone learned about each member, and how it may help strengthen the team.

Results

Participation in this activity builds capacity for the team to make difficult decisions by helping team members express vulnerability and find commonalities. And while the emphasis may be for new team members, veteran members will benefit from participation as well.

Summary

New superintendents and school board members come to their positions with both excitement and trepidation. The qualities that will ultimately emerge as the individuals move into their governance and leadership roles will largely be determined by how each is introduced to them and supported during those first critical months in his or her position. A well-planned and orchestrated orientation program will help both superintendents and school board members ease into their positions.

Induction programs help support more trusting relationships that translate to team effectiveness. Minimally, an atmosphere of mutual respect for the role each team member plays is essential for the team to function effectively. Additionally, within the umbrella of mutual respect there needs to be a pledge that an honest, regular communication exchange will be part of the ongoing orientation program and the broader commitment to appropriate induction activities.

Chapter 3

Team Members' Roles and Responsibilities

Who does what? This question is simple and might at first imply an equally simple answer in response. However, when it comes to the school board–superintendent relationship, this is not an unassuming question at all. Matching job responsibilities to expectations is not easily accomplished unless all parties have a thorough understanding of roles and responsibilities from an oversight position, in the case of a school board member, as well as an administrative or management position, for superintendents. A thorough understanding and agreement on the roles each plays in district governance helps to ensure that future disagreements are relegated to matters of fact, culture, philosophy, or values, and not who is in a position of authority.

Most superintendents and school board members have heard this expression or its equivalent at some point: "School boards make policy; superintendents run schools." Although this time-honored phrase is essentially correct, the interrelationship between the school board's and superintendent's roles is not as strictly categorized as that expression suggests. In the 21st century governance relationship, often viewed as a board–superintendent team, the lines that define how boards and superintendents interact are often blurred—becoming more interwoven along the edges of each's distinctive, and sometimes more traditional, responsibilities. For example, it is true that school boards are responsible for policy, but rarely do school boards meet solely to develop policy. Rather, policy development is often the product of the superintendent's suggestions, and the superintendent (or in some instances the school district's legal counsel) routinely reviews the policies before the superintendent presents them to the school board for initial review and subsequent adoption. Likewise, superintendents often consult with school boards before making strategic management decisions. Although policy serves to regulate and guide the school personnel as they perform their roles and responsibilities, it does not even remotely describe all that school board members do, the kinds of issues that cross their desks, or how they routinely interact with superintendents and school personnel.

This chapter will guide teams in working through issues of role and responsibility overlap, through carefully considering the question, "Who does what?"

Role and Responsibility Overlap

As we noted in figure I.1 (page 2), considerable overlap exists between the roles and responsibilities of school boards and superintendents. Confusion about this overlap can lead to awkward governance situations and unnecessary conflict between the parties. It is not uncommon for such conflict to occur between boards and superintendents after board elections or following superintendent changes. Unfortunately, school boards often become involved in situations that are not appropriately their concern, and superintendents occasionally supersede their authority without board approval. A lack of understanding, a misunderstanding, or an intentional act beyond the position's traditional, accepted parameters is the root.

Similarly, boards and superintendents working with only a superficial understanding of each side's expectations soon find conflict, each one believing the other is interfering or acting within areas beyond its specific role and responsibilities. From personal observations over several years, these incursions by the superintendent into areas of school board responsibility or the intrusion of school board members into areas of superintendent responsibility are not only possible, they are probable. The resulting friction is aggravating and possibly confusing to other school employees, and if not addressed it can damage the school board–superintendent relationship.

The good news is that these intentional incursions into areas of responsibility that appropriately belong to someone else are completely avoidable. However, it requires early, frequent, and deliberate conversations between the superintendent and the school board regarding roles and responsibilities. These conversations must be more than just reviewing the district's organizational chart to see who reports to whom, how the line of authority is structured, or what the job descriptions say. Each of these options has value and provides useful information, but the conversations should ultimately be more philosophical, requiring a discussion of implied, positional, and real authority. Topics of conversation should include distinguishing between administrative and managerial responsibilities, which are clearly the superintendent's responsibility, and governance oversight responsibility, which exclusively belongs to the school board. While these textbook responsibility definitions are widely accepted as the optimal positional and operational guidelines within an effective school board–superintendent model, they are largely self-imposed. It is each school board–superintendent team's responsibility to define who does what and to require voluntary limitations from its members on the kinds of activities and actions they will intentionally follow if they are to move forward as a team.

Ongoing Delegation of Responsibility Conversation

It is critical to hold a *who does what* conversation whenever the dynamics of the school board–superintendent team change. Certainly, when a school board is interviewing superintendent applicants, this question should be part of the interview process, and if the school board does not broach the subject, the candidate should. This intentional conversation has the potential to safeguard the board–superintendent relationship; it is obviously more advisable to spend time discussing the question during the application process than having to divert potential conflict later in the relationship due to misunderstandings regarding the relational boundaries. However, it is also essential to revisit the topic anytime the dynamics in the boardroom change—for example, when new board members are seated, or when there is a new superintendent elected. An open, honest conversation is necessary to understand and agree on who is going to be responsible for what, as well as how and when either side can and should engage the other before a decision is made. A successful conversation should define the board–superintendent relationship going forward and deepen the concept of *team*.

What are some *who does what* questions that should be part of this ongoing conversation? The following list contains some examples, although it is far from a finite list. In some respects, the kinds of questions addressed are those that a person would normally expect from new board members when they assume office. However, veteran members and superintendents ask these questions just as often. Representative questions surrounding boards and superintendents might be as follows.

- Should the school board be involved in hiring personnel other than the superintendent?
- What is the process for approving and paying claims?
- Who is responsible for speaking to the media?
- Who addresses public concerns with school personnel?
- Who determines the meeting agenda?

Breaking down the conversation into manageable segments is important if the conversation is to be productive. First, consider the *what* in the questions the team is asking—what tasks does the school board, superintendent, or both need to complete? Looking at the questions in the preceding list, the *what* topics are: (1) hiring personnel, (2) paying claims, (3) speaking to the media, (4) addressing public concerns, and (5) setting board meeting agendas. Stripped of any additional information, there is nothing threatening about any of these issues. However, when the team begins discussing *who* is responsible for each of these and how to accomplish each, opinions can differ. The following section discusses the complexity surrounding the *who* question.

Role Designation

It is necessary that both board members and their superintendent agree, philosophically and practically, on the role of board members and superintendents. Even if there has been a successful discussion of *what* needs to be done, determining *who* is responsible can quickly turn into a turf war. The resolutions for potential authority disagreements are more readily determined by asking a simple question: "Is this issue one of *management* or one of *governance oversight*?" This question speaks directly to superintendents and school boards because, although their roles are complementary, they are not identical.

The school board member's role is one of governance oversight. Education as a profession dictates that employees must have appropriate education and licensure to serve in teaching and administrative contract roles. As board members come from all backgrounds, many of which do not include licensure or studies in education, this means that board members do not operate in an administrative capacity. We can see this reflected in the fact that school board members are generally not actively engaged in school-related issues on a daily basis in their role as board members. Most board members have careers outside of public education; consequently, they only brush against public education at regular intervals, peering in to ensure the school district is operating in accordance to policy and established expectations based on the culture and climate of the particular community where the school district is established. They act as check and balance between state and federal regulations and community expectations.

School boards have one of the most difficult jobs in public education: they provide governance oversight for everything within the organization, yet they manage nothing. Board members who understand their role and responsibility is not an administrative one, but rather one of governance oversight, are more apt to refrain from involvement in the everyday details of school operation, preferring to adopt a more strategic focus. This forever-watching, but hands-off posture enables and empowers school staff members to manage the district operations according to established policies and agreed-on expectations.

Superintendents, while working closely with the school board, have responsibilities that mirror those of the CEO of a traditional business or corporation. In most instances, the superintendent is responsible for the effective management of a multimillion-dollar educational enterprise. Schools districts are often one of the largest employers, if not the largest, in the district. They are often the largest food provider, and they manage the largest transportation operation in their communities. The entire school district's operation is the superintendent's sole responsibility and, while a superintendent may ultimately delegate management responsibility to other key personnel in the district, he or she still remains accountable for the overall operation. Essentially, this means that if something goes wrong, it is the superintendent's fault.

Accountability for the overall operation is an expectation that superintendents willingly assume and one that the board should never want to undertake. In the ideal line of authority, every school employee in the district is ultimately accountable to the superintendent, while the superintendent alone is accountable to the school board. Perhaps one way to describe the accountability equation is that the superintendent is accountable for a school district's operation and the school board is accountable for how the school district operates. And while the roles are complex, effective board–superintendent teams can operate successfully with these understandings.

In these complementary roles, both superintendents and school board members are inexorably aligned within the public education governance structure. There have been many things written about how the relationship between superintendents and school board members should be structured, but there is one practical example that explains it better than all the rhetoric. At most school board meetings, there is a long table, perhaps in a U or V shape, and all the board members' chairs are placed on one side of that table. Additionally, the superintendent's chair is most often positioned alongside board members' chairs. Everyone else sits on the opposite side of the table in front of those chairs. If nothing else, the example should speak volumes regarding the nature of the school board–superintendent relationship: they are both on the same side of the governance table. Everyone else—teachers, support staff, community members, business partners, and so on—are on the opposite side of the governance team in the school district. This does not imply that they are antagonists, only that the responsibility for governance exclusively belongs to the superintendent and school board. Everyone else works or operates within the structure that the school board–superintendent governance structure defines.

Recall the *what* examples discussed earlier in the chapter considering the responsibility and accountability descriptions. The *who* question should now be more easily identified. Remember, the question of *who* is one of responsibility, not necessarily authority. In this situation, *authority* pertains to the power or influence a person has over others, while *responsibility* speaks to personal or positional performance obligations. Reviewing the earlier examples, we could reach the following conclusions based on the management and governance oversight definitions used earlier.

- **Hiring personnel:** This is strictly a management issue, and hence, the superintendent's responsibility. While school boards may be keenly interested in the type of individuals hired, they are not responsible for those individuals' performance—the superintendent is. School boards should not confuse their legal responsibility as contract providers with the direct responsibility for those employees' performance. Since school board members are not involved in the school district's daily operation, it is presumptuous to assert that they are in a better position to determine staffing needs than the superintendent hired to manage the district.

- **Paying claims:** This is both a management and governance oversight responsibility. However, management bears the greater burden. It is management's responsibility (the superintendent) to operate according to the policies governing expenditures, and it is the governance oversight body's responsibility (the school board) to verify and approve those expenditures.

- **Speaking to the media:** This is primarily a management responsibility. The superintendent or his or her designee is appropriately responsible for communicating with the media for all issues that are school district-related. The school board, however, has a responsibility to address the media on those issues of interest that pertain to the positions and views adopted by the school board. (Such issues could be results of board action, controversial issues within the district, building programs, or matters involving board procedure, among others.)

- **Addressing public concerns with school district issues:** Management is clearly the right choice for addressing concerns. It is not uncommon for community concerns to be conveyed to the school board, either at a public meeting or with individual members privately; however, individual school board members have no authority to address issues outside of a public meeting. Their authority is only realized when they are in a publicly advertised and convened meeting of the entire school board. Separately, board members are powerless from a legal or ethical perspective.

- **Setting board meeting agendas:** Management bears the greater burden because the superintendent is responsible for the district's daily operation. As such, superintendents understand the importance for bringing specific agenda items to the governing body's attention at certain points during the year. This does not mean that school boards are left without a voice in their own meetings. Board members can bring agenda items to the entire board's attention for discussion and subsequent action. However, addressing those items that are germane for the district's smooth operation and are important to address in a timely matter always takes precedence.

Reviewing the *who* responsibilities appears to place a greater emphasis on management (the responsibility of the superintendent), but it must be remembered that the question of *who* is one of responsibility, not authority. Being responsible for both qualitative and quantitative results within roles and responsibilities is a performance obligation of an individual authorized (directed) to meet those expectations. That direction or authorization may be expressed through specific board action, through policy, or as a response to an element within a job description.

Role and Responsibility Conflicts

This chapter has stated only a few of the *who does what* questions that could be asked in a school board–superintendent conversation. From these questions, it is easy to comprehend how a school board–superintendent team could mistakenly confuse authority with responsibility. Without an intentional discussion and a firm regard for the responsibility that comes with position and job descriptions, superintendents and school board members are more apt to infringe on each other's areas of responsibility. The best preventative is the *who does what* discussion, with the key objective being an early and mutual understanding between the superintendent and school board regarding each other's role in the operation and decision-making tenets of the school district.

Each side of the governance equation—management and governance oversight—must be clearly delineated and the roles within those lines observed and respected. This relationship is at the pinnacle of the school district's real and implied line of authority, and repeated failures on either side, breaching the mutual respect at this high level of responsibility and authority, invariably send shock waves cascading throughout the district. It is important to note that it is usually *repeated* failures that lead to conflicts in the school board–superintendent team, rather than one-off mistakes, particularly if the mistake occurs unintentionally and is without malice. Honorable intent at the root of irresponsible actions can be overlooked or forgiven, but not repeatedly. Single infractions can occur innocently, but severe or repeated occurrences clearly show disrespect for the other side's authority. Consequently, the respect that either side has for the other will be significantly damaged if the infraction is large enough or if it is consistently repeated. Unless immediate action is taken to acknowledge and repair the breach, the damage may ultimately be too severe to sustain the relationship. Unaddressed trespasses can lead to all of the maladies associated with a toxic work environment at the leadership level, which often results in the exit of the superintendent from the district.

Obviously, preventing damage is preferable to repairing it. The best preventative is an open, honest dialogue of expectations for authority and responsibility. Revisiting that conversation at routine intervals is advisable, but especially when the boardroom dynamic changes or when a new situation in the district demands clarifying who does what.

Professional Development Activity on Roles and Responsibilities

This activity helps team members clarify their roles and responsibilities. It uses open-ended questions to encourage an honest and open discussion about who does what among team members.

Time Frame

This activity should take approximately sixty minutes.

Materials

The team needs a facilitator, a recorder, the list of questions, pens or pencils and paper, and a whiteboard and whiteboard markers (or easel, chart paper, and markers).

Process

After identifying a facilitator and a recorder—someone who will list responses on the whiteboard—the team should do the following.

1. As a team, review the following three questions.

    ◆ What issues should the superintendent address without consulting the school board for its opinion or approval?

    ◆ What issues or decisions should the school board entertain without the superintendent's input?

    ◆ What issues require collaboration between the board and superintendent before any action is pursued?

2. Individually, each member should take ten minutes to respond to each question, noting responses he or she is comfortable sharing with the entire team.

3. Next, the facilitator should encourage members to share their responses with two to three neighboring team members. Members can ask questions to clarify but must not judge the other team members' responses as right or wrong.

4. The facilitator should then bring the team back together and invite responses to the first question. The recorder should list responses to the question so that the collection of responses is viewable by all.

5. The facilitator then leads a discussion on key points of commonality and disagreement. The team continues discussion until it finds a level of consensus. If key points of disagreement remain, plan additional discussion for another time until the team reaches consensus regarding the question and disagreement.

6. The facilitator then addresses the second and third questions individually, using a similar format for sharing and clarifying responses among team members. Again, the recorder should list responses to the second and third questions so that the collection of responses is viewable by all.

7. The facilitator concludes the activity by asking if there is anything else to discuss about the overall questions and responses that team members did not have the opportunity to share.

8. The recorder, at his or her earliest convenience, formalizes the final agreements by typing them into a document and distributing them to team members. This will serve as an important reminder of the agreements, which the team can easily utilize as needed.

Results

Participation in this activity encourages honest and open discussion and consensus about school board–superintendent team members' varying roles and responsibilities.

Summary

The seemingly simple question of *who does what* is actually a complex question for the school board–superintendent team, and an agreeable response may at first be difficult. Articulating expectations for team members is not easy without a better understanding of roles and responsibilities from a governance oversight position as well as an administrative or management position. Similarly, initial efforts should focus on the *what* expectations for the team, to deepen understanding about *who* is responsible.

A thoughtful discussion and questioning strategy will assist team members to explore the *who does what* implications for team members. An emphasis on clarifying *who* and *what* issues will strengthen team effectiveness by minimizing role and responsibility overlap and proactively delegating responsibility and authority for key topics the team must address, including hiring personnel, paying claims, speaking to the media, addressing public concerns, and setting board meeting agendas.

Chapter 4
Effective Communication and a Unified Voice

This chapter deals with two very important topics: (1) the art of effective superintendent and school board member communication and (2) how to speak with one unified voice. Although the effective communication section applies to the school board–superintendent team, speaking with one voice is predominantly aimed at the collective voice of school boards.

There is ample literature (Conger & Kanungo, 1998; Covey, 2006; Daft, 2005; Kouzes & Posner, 2003; Mayer, 2011) regarding the hallmarks of effective communication, and there will be several references from some of those resources. However, it needs to be stressed that the highlighted literature is only a fraction of the research that supports the material provided in this chapter. Speaking with one voice is a much narrower topic, particularly with respect to school board members serving on the same board. Consequently, vetting each area thoroughly is preferable before attempting to show the importance of the board members' relationships. This chapter will address this important merger and the subsequent communication of individual thoughts and ideas that ultimately represents the single governance voice of the school board.

The Art of Effective Communication

Merely transmitting information does not indicate that communication has transpired, and neither does the receipt of information. This is because, to the surprise of many, the transmission and receipt of information does not mean that a correct interpretation of information exists. For communication to occur, there must be "components of sending, receiving, and feedback" (Daft, 2005, p. 344), and the individual or group that is conveying information relies on feedback to ensure that the transmitted information has been correctly interpreted. Effective communication cannot exist without sending information, receiving information, or giving feedback;

and it is important to begin with this prescription of communication to ground the rest of this commentary.

While the general information regarding communication is applicable in all circumstances, there are different expectations for different communications, depending on various roles and positions within an organization. Leaders in the school district have one primary communication goal, and managers have another. The communication from the leader most often addresses a desired result, while a manager's communication most often directs who will act, how the task will be accomplished, and the desired result. Subsequently, the styles of leader communication and manager communication, as well as a third unique style, charismatic communication, are quite different in purpose and usage.

Leadership-Style Communication

Leadership-style communication is different from manager-style communication since it concentrates on building trust and gaining commitment to the organization's vision. Leaders are *big-picture* people (Daft, 2005) who understand that their role is to communicate through a visionary lens, keeping people focused on the organization's future. Communication leaders "understand that unless they communicate and share information with their constituents, few will take much interest in what is going on" (Kouzes & Posner, 2003, p. 172). As an example, a superintendent may communicate to his or her school board regarding a particular facet of a building or renovation project by stating, "The project is proceeding on schedule, and the much-needed improvements it promises are expected to play a major role in the school board's goal of improving student achievement to exceed state standards over three years."

Managerial-Style Communication

Managers, on the other hand, are information processors, predominantly relying on data and ideas and communicating these to others (Daft, 2005). These are the individuals who direct daily activities throughout the school district, the classrooms, and the district's support areas (transportation, food services, maintenance, and so on). Using the same example of a building or renovation project, a manager might communicate to his or her subordinates in this manner: "The building project is on schedule. Within two months, we need to have a developed plan showing how we will orchestrate facility use for maximum results. Please have your plan suggestions prepared for our next team meeting."

Charismatic-Style Communication

A third communication style, building on the strengths of managerial and leadership styles, can also arise—the uncommon, yet desirable, style known as *charismatic communication*. As Jay Conger and Rabindra Kanungo (1998) note in their research, charismatic leaders possess a high need to change the status quo, have a vision that is highly different from the status quo, are counter-normative, and have the power to influence. That observation is also supported in more recent observations (Spahr, 2016).

Teams should use charismatic communication with caution. It has the potential to bring too much attention on an individual team member or even the team itself. With charisma, the communication may be inspiring or motivating, but success may be associated with those communicating charismatically and not with the broader group of stakeholders in the district who are also contributing to success. Over time, an overreliance on those communicating charismatically may occur, devaluing others' contributions.

Using the previous example again, a self-serving communication from a charismatic leader might be expressed like this: "I am happy to say that the project I have fought so hard to make available to you is on schedule. I am so thankful for the privilege of bringing you this great opportunity and grateful that the school board also grasped the wisdom of my recommendation." An example where the communication would serve to engage the group might be, "The project we have all been waiting for is well underway and on schedule. The opportunities this project will afford is a result of the board's support for our school and for your recommendations."

Naturally, school board members and superintendents should display differing communication styles, depending on their unique roles and responsibilities. The following sections discuss the three communication styles in the context of both superintendents and school board members.

Superintendent Communication

The superintendent's artful application of communication requires knowing when to communicate as the manager and when to communicate as the leader. Truthfully, he or she must be able to do both to be effective, but every communication must begin with a desire to make the right impression. That means ensuring that communication is not misunderstood (Covey, 2006).

Superintendents should consider levels of administration in the school district when deciding which communication style to use. In a small district, a superintendent may wear any number of administrative hats, while in others there can be multiple administrative tiers. These differences dictate the superintendent's ratio of leader-to-manager communication, but are completely dependent upon administrative resource, which is typically determined by district size. Not every superintendent successfully transitions from a small district to a large one or vice versa, not because he or she does not understand the superintendent's role from a practical standpoint, but because the leader-to-manager communication requirements are radically different from each other. Consequently, any superintendent moving from a large district to a small one or from a small district to one that is larger must acknowledge that the move necessitates a change in the manner in which he or she communicates within the district.

Regardless of district size, it is reasonable that the superintendent's communication with school board members will be that of a leader, connecting shared information and data with the district's goals and vision. Although the superintendent will convey a variety of information, facts, ideas, and so on, it is always with a focus on the school district and its pursuit of the district vision, or accomplishing a district goal. The superintendent is the school board's primary source of pertinent information regarding the school district. As such, the superintendent should provide the vast majority of information regarding district performance, education initiatives, business-decision rationale, and so on, to board members, and supplement this with leadership-style communication that connects this information with his or her goals for the school district. In other words, in addition to communicating important information relating to district performance, it is equally important for the superintendent to communicate how that performance helps the district to realize its goals and objectives aligning with strategic initiatives.

Transparency—openly sharing information with all people who have reason to access that information—is an important factor of the superintendent's leadership-style communication. For example, when a superintendent answers one board member's question, it is reasonable to conclude that the superintendent will also share the same information with all board members. This ensures each board member has the opportunity to benefit from the superintendent's response to the question.

In communication with subordinates, the superintendent should appropriately model the communication style of a manager, conveying necessary information and ideas for consideration and follow-through. However, the superintendent must also inspire and encourage followers through a leader communication style as well. Understanding the overall purpose, the *why* behind the directives, invites followers to join the purpose and to be part of the overall plan to support the organizational vision.

Managerial-style communication and leadership-style communication are very different, but both are essential to the superintendent role. A superintendent who only communicates in one style or the other may insult, disenfranchise, or provide insufficient direction to one group or the other. Over time, each is equally disastrous to career longevity.

Charismatic communication is always beneficial when using it to inspire or motivate the district. However, charismatic leaders can appear arrogant and unresponsive to their subordinates. It is then that their communication may appear to be more self-serving, and they may lose the respect of their followers.

School Board Communication

Board communications, on the other hand, are divided into two categories: intra-school board–superintendent team, and public. Both emanate from leadership-style communication to match the governance role of the school board. Nonetheless, for very practical reasons, communication within the team and communication with the public require distinct differences. Board members must have a good, working understanding of their position as a public official, as well as their role as one of several members that comprise the governing body, and hence the need to ultimately speak with one unified voice. In discussing the school board's use of effective communication, we will first consider communication within the school board–superintendent team and then discuss communication with the public.

Communication With the Superintendent

When board members have questions for the superintendent, they must have a mechanism in place to allow for a meaningful exchange of information. This mechanism may include email, texts, phone calls, or face-to-face meetings. It is important that this mechanism include a provision for transparency since, as stated earlier, the superintendent should not share information with one board member and intentionally withhold that information from the others. In other words, *what one board member knows, all board members know*. It will be helpful for board members to put procedures in place to avoid conflict and to ensure that communication within the school board–superintendent team is transparent.

Conflicts in school board communication often occur when members adopt a different communication style. While board member communications should follow the leadership style of communication, it is not uncommon for board members to stray into a managerial style. This frequently causes problems because, although the board is technically the superintendent's employer or boss, the ideal relationship is complementary or collegial. Consequently, board members who adopt managerial-style communication can do significant damage to the relationship. Remember, managerial communication is primarily to direct the daily activity of the district (Daft, 2005), and managing the district is outside of the school board's responsibility. Being responsible for the management of the district is much different from responsibly managing the district. Effective school board–superintendent teams deal with this via an open dialogue permitting each side to speak freely about turf concerns before they escalate.

Board members' intraschool board–superintendent communications are generally private, one-on-one conversations that go relatively unnoticed. However, when a school board convenes in its official capacity, communication is public and the method of communication must change.

Communication With the Public

Board members' communication to the public can occur in two situations: (1) when conducting board business in a setting to which the public is invited, and (2) when speaking directly to the public. Board meetings are rule-governed events in which there is typically a formal order of business and a boardroom protocol that supplants board communications occurring between meetings. In conversations prior to meetings, to which the public is not privy, all board members generally have the liberty to casually ask questions and receive answers individually. These communications are often exploratory, information-gathering exchanges that help to ensure that board members enter into future decision making adequately prepared. However, boards that convene in a public meeting must be more guarded with communication. That is not to suggest that it must not be open or forthcoming, only that it is important that questions and responses be particularly phrased to prevent the public from misunderstanding. Most states have statutory language that, with few exceptions, does not allow school boards to meet privately. Not choosing words carefully when the audience in the boardroom may not have the complete background on a situation, or leaving listeners without the same background knowledge as the board to interpret what a statement means, can create a communication nightmare.

Choosing language carefully and providing consistent information to the public is never more important than when the school board is addressing controversial or high-profile issues in the school district. During these times, we suggest that the school board appoint a board spokesperson. It then becomes the spokesperson's obligation to address any formal inquiries requiring a board response by sharing the information the board wishes to release. Questions from the community or media outlets regarding consolidation, school closings or redistricting, reductions in force, and so on call for this. The obvious value is that a single board member, acting on behalf of the entire board, is more apt to consistently and clearly share the same information in response to multiple inquiries, whereas answers from individual board members to the same issue have a greater propensity to vary from one member to another. Even if all members agree on an issue, an individual's creative license or embellishment opens opportunities for misunderstanding.

There is never a reason for an individual board member to communicate a presumed board position to a patron, media outlets, a school employee, or anyone else without the board's authority (Mayer, 2011). Additionally, although there are obvious practical and ethical reasons individual board members should not engage in personal communications regarding school district business or issues, it must be a self-governing practice. No board member has specific authority over another member. Consequently, the majority of restrictions and rules the board adheres to, the manner in which the board members conduct business, and how they communicate in public are completely voluntary.

Equally important is whom the board appoints as its official spokesperson. Quite often, that de facto responsibility falls to the board president, but the designated spokesperson can be anyone serving on the board, or it can change depending on circumstance. What is important is that the board's official spokesperson be comfortable in that role and that he or she is careful to share only the position the board has assumed on an issue or only the information the board intends to release. In this sense, the official board spokesperson is the board's authorized messenger—nothing more.

The official board spokesperson should deal only with matters pertaining to the board's governance oversight responsibility. Matters pertaining to school district issues, from an administrative perspective, should be referred to the school district's official spokesperson. That person will vary from school district to school district, but quite often, that responsibility falls to the superintendent. Examples where the school might desire to channel communications through an official spokesperson are temporary school closings; emergencies, accidents, or both; school personnel issues; and so on. The general public is not likely to remember whom they should contact for each issue, so it is important that school board members and school administrators understand who is responsible to speak to an inquiry and can direct the concern appropriately without undue commentary. This helps to ensure consistent communication and maintain the communication demarcation line. These opportune teaching-by-example moments with community members perfectly illustrate the shared respect between the administrative and governing branches of the school district.

Obviously, not every circumstance demands questions be directed to and answered by the board's official spokesperson. The official spokesperson practice is to minimize opportunities for public or patron misunderstandings during those instances when the board is dealing with high-profile or otherwise emotionally charged issues. It is important that board members can remain focused on the issue without the distraction of fielding questions from reporters or concerned citizens. Both groups are important, and the board should never avoid addressing their concerns. However, *how* and *who* addresses them can establish a professional working relationship that allows for effective communication without jeopardizing board performance.

One Unified Voice

School boards can meet in special meetings, committee meetings, executive sessions, and public hearings, and all of these have a peculiar communication format reflecting each meeting category. However, since regular meetings are convened on a regular basis, it is this meeting communication that we will address in this section. All other meetings will utilize a variation of this communication pattern, with some liberties that mirror the board's character, traditional practice, and the community culture and climate. However, in every instance, the superintendent and/or the superintendent's designee should be present at every meeting, regardless of meeting type. The only exception to that is when the school board meets to officially conduct the superintendent's evaluation.

The school board, superintendent, and members of the general public attend regular communication meetings and follow a prescribed order that allows a board to sequentially proceed through its meeting agenda. These meetings only occasionally offer opportunities for communication of new information, although there are opportunities for that possibility before each decision is rendered (assuming most boards follow a hybrid version of Robert's Rules of Order [Robert, 1978/1915] that allows for speaking to a motion before voting). New information can be presented at that time, but that is usually the exception rather than the rule. More often, the board has already received a packet of information from their superintendent communicating the appropriate background information for each agenda item and his or her administrative recommendation. Likewise, board members have an opportunity to address the information and recommendation with the superintendent before the meeting if there are questions or disagreements with the superintendent's recommendation. Nothing prohibits a board member from conducting their own research; however, it should be used as a matter of information in the communications between the superintendent and the board member before the meeting. This is a responsible intraschool board–superintendent conversation that necessarily precedes regular meetings. Consequently, at regular meetings there is little, if any, additional information that needs to occur for the school board and superintendent to each fulfill the responsibilities of their respective positions.

Because regular meetings are held in public, and the public is granted an opportunity to observe the school board and superintendent as they publicly deliberate and act, the public may be under the impression that it has legal standing to weigh in on the decision-making process. Attendees may try to use these meetings as a time to make comments, offer advice, disagree with recommendations, and so on. While there can be some benefit for the board (typically the board president presiding at the meeting) or superintendent to briefly review the background of an agenda item prior to asking for a motion to move the agenda item to a decision, the board president must be clear that this is a one-way communication process and that the board alone has responsibility for making decisions. Although it is within the board's purview to entertain communication exchanges with whomever it chooses, the board must be extremely careful not to jeopardize its authority and obligation as decision makers based on possible repercussions from public attendance fallout at regular meetings.

At all times, school boards should agree and adhere to a meeting protocol that provides for the routine execution of the school district's business to ensure they speak with one voice. The board should not surrender that responsibility, regardless of public pressure. This enforces a well-known anonymous phrase that states, "School board meetings are not public meetings, they are meetings held in public." Of course, most people can think of an exception or a time when the board was well served by a comment a patron contributed during a discussion before the board voted. We will not discount that those instances occur and still will occur. However, if the superintendent has exercised due diligence by providing the appropriate background information and a recommendation data support—and if the board has thoroughly reviewed that information, asked any questions, posed any concerns prior to the meeting that the superintendent responded to before arriving at the business meeting—the opportunity for an eleventh-hour revelation that effectively nullifies the recommendation before the board becomes less likely. Ultimately, teams should strive for meeting communications that are timely, appropriate, and necessary for furthering the work of school governance.

There are always questions regarding how best to communicate, both for intraschool board–superintendent and public communications. School districts have an array of communication methods at their disposal, including:

- Web-based platforms such as the district web page
- Email
- Social media applications, like Facebook, Skype, Twitter, Snapchat, Instagram, and so on
- Face-to-face meetings
- Phone calls or conference calls, like FaceTime or GoToMeeting
- Hand-written or typed documents

Each of these, as well as others that are available, has benefits for both one-way and two-way communications, some that are more preferable than others under particular circumstances.

It is also important that boards and superintendents consider the legal implications of the communication method they use. Legal considerations include ensuring compliance to statutory rules, and providing guidelines for transparency and liability considerations. Communicating private information regarding school personnel or students, public notice of meetings, and emergency notices each have their own prescribed form and rule for communicating that must be followed.

Professional Development Activity on Communication

This activity allows team members to deepen their understanding of leadership-style, managerial-style, and charismatic-style communication. It helps team members identify the advantages, disadvantages, and skills associated with each style.

Time Frame

This activity requires thirty to forty-five minutes to complete.

Materials

The team will need a facilitator, a copy of figure 4.1 containing a description of the three communication styles (page 54), and a whiteboard and markers.

Leadership-Style Communication

Leadership-style communication concentrates on building trust and gaining commitment to the organization's vision. Leaders are big-picture people (Daft, 2005) who understand that their role is to communicate through a visionary lens, keeping people focused on the organization's future. Communication leaders "understand that unless they communicate and share information with their constituents, few will take much interest in what is going on" (Kouzes & Posner, 2003, p. 172). As an example, a superintendent may communicate to his or her school board regarding a particular facet of a building or renovation project by stating, "The project is proceeding on schedule, and the much-needed improvements it promises are expected to play a major role in the school board's goal of improving student achievement to exceed state standards over three years."

Managerial-Style Communication

Managers, on the other hand, are information processors, predominantly relying on data and ideas and communicating these to others (Daft, 2005). These are the individuals who direct daily activities throughout the school

---

district, the classrooms, and the district's support areas (transportation, food services, maintenance, and so on). Using the same example of a building or renovation project, a manager might communicate to his or her subordinates in this manner: "The building project is on schedule. Within two months, we need to have a developed plan showing how we will orchestrate facility use for maximum results. Please have your plan suggestions prepared for our next team meeting."

Charismatic-Style Communication

As Jay Conger and Rabindra Kanungo note (1998), charismatic leaders possess a high need to change the status quo, have a vision that is highly different from the status quo, are counter-normative, and have the power to influence. Teams should use charismatic communication with caution. This style has the potential to bring too much attention on an individual team member or even the team itself. With charisma, the communication may be inspiring or motivating, but success may be associated with those communicating charismatically and not with the broader group of stakeholders in the district who are also contributing to success. Over time, an overreliance on those communicating charismatically may occur, devaluing others' contributions.

A self-serving communication from a charismatic leader might be expressed like this: "I am happy to say that the project I have fought so hard to make available to you is on schedule. I am so thankful for the privilege of bringing you this great opportunity and grateful that the school board also grasped the wisdom of my recommendation." An example where the communication would serve to engage the group might be, "The project we have all been waiting for is well underway and on schedule. The opportunities this project will afford is a result of the board's support for our school and for your recommendations."

Figure 4.1: The three styles of communication.

*Visit **go.SolutionTree.com/leadership** to download a free reproducible version of this figure.*

Process

This activity may be completed as a team, in small groups, or individually.

After reviewing the leadership, managerial, and charismatic communication styles this chapter describes (see figure 4.1, page 54), teams should do the following.

1. State what other characteristics they believe further define the three communication styles. The facilitator should keep a visible list for the team to view as the activity continues.

2. Review the list of communication skills in figure 4.2 (page 56) and determine which style of communication each list item is associated with.

- Asks relevant questions
- After asking a question, maintains an open mind about the response and is not defensive
- Discerns between actual questions and value-laden statements; minimizes the use of statements
- Challenges ideas without intimidating
- Understands the right place and time for a conversation
- Listens carefully for the true intent of a message and weighs it against nonverbal messaging
- Looks for meaningful nonverbal communication
- Shows an interest in others and maintains eye contact
- Looks beyond a speaker's words and is sensitive to his or her emotions and feelings
- Listens to the whole message
- Avoids rambling
- Works on message clarity and delivery
- Relies on facts and evidence
- Checks to see if the audience has heard the board's intended message
- Tries to avoid words that are all-inclusive and overly generalizing (for instance, *all*, *never*, *everybody*, or *always*)
- Speaks with confidence but does not assume he or she is always right
- Relies on expert authority, minimizing feedback
- Uses well-prepared sound bites
- Responds respectfully, choosing words that will not incite or elevate a situation but rather show understanding even when additional information is needed
- Is open to constructive criticism and other ideas, especially if the data are inconclusive

Figure 4.2: Communication skills.

*Visit **go.SolutionTree.com/leadership** to download a free reproducible version of this figure.*

3. Discuss, as a group, each person's responses. Use the following to guide the conversation.

    ◆ Were there differences among team members? Discuss why.

    ◆ Did any team members place one skill in multiple styles? Which skill and styles?

    ◆ Does each member's dominant communication style change as the team agenda changes?

◆ What style is most needed from the superintendent at this time? What style is needed from the board? What style overall is needed from the school board–superintendent team? Is it the same or different for the superintendent, the board, and the overall team? Why or why not?

Results

Participation in this activity reinforces the three communication styles' strengths and challenges and enhances the team's unified voice.

As the team reviews the professional development activity, it may seem there is an inordinate amount of information to consider and to keep track of, at least initially. However, it is important to remember that the school board–superintendent team changes with regularity, most frequently as some board members leave at the end of each member's term and others replace them. Considering that this opportunity for change may occur every two or three years—election and appointments—then team members can readily understand that this turnover requires a constant learning and review process. This review process ensures that board and superintendent communications are not only constantly meeting their intercommunication expectations but also providing an effective communication channel to their constituents and staff members.

Summary

An effective school board–superintendent team understands the importance of speaking with one voice. The chosen communication style of the board and superintendent has power to influence the team. Understanding the basics of leadership-style, managerial-style, or charismatic communication facilitates improved communication among team members. The professional development activity facilitates deeper understanding of the three communication styles and proactively builds capacity for team member changes and their impact on effective communication. A single voice from the school board–superintendent team can effectively direct, inform, and inspire those within the team and those to whom the team is ultimately responsible when expressed appropriately and responsibly.

Chapter 5
Team Decision Making

A board member's individual role in decision making and, subsequently, the board's aggregate responsibility for making decisions are some of the least-discussed tenets of boardmanship. Adding to those responsibilities are a myriad of issues, each requiring board approval in the form of a decision before the school district can proceed. Additionally, the superintendent assumes an important role in decision making as well. In this chapter, we will address how board members make decisions and the superintendent's role in that process; however, the same process we describe for school board members is applicable to the decision-making process the superintendent and his or her administrative team employs.

It is important to understand the line of authority to establish the flow of accountability in decision making. In terms of hierarchy within a school district, school board members are at the top, followed by the superintendent, then other key central office personnel, and finally building administrators, managers, and so on. However, practically speaking, the school board–superintendent team operates as a single decision-making entity. Within this entity, each individual plays an integral role in the process and, if absent, can potentially compromise the entire process to the school district's detriment. These roles, while integral, are also distinct, emanating from different responsibility.

What are the different decisions school boards make? Generically, we might suggest that anything requiring a formal vote qualifies as a board decision, but a state's legislative process predetermines some decisions. Technically, those are also decisions, but they are decisions of compliance to a legislative directive; consequently, these are low on the list of decisions boards make, even though they often have a tremendous impact on the educational process and environment. Other decisions involve the payment for services (claims), permission to pursue specific action items, the concurrence to incur future obligations, and a host of additional items.

When we speak of decisions and decision making, we are referring to those decisions that are primarily within the board's purview that have reasonable options to consider. Ironically, when reviewing the literature for a school board's or superintendent's decision-making process, there is little that addresses the issue exclusively regarding school boards or superintendents. See the chapter "The Board as Decision Maker" in the National School Boards Association's ([NSBA], 2006) *Becoming a Better Board Member*, which summarizes decision making into a six-step model.

1. Define the problem.

2. Gather information on the problem.

3. Get the superintendent's recommendation and consider any alternative recommendation he or she may offer (for example, input from the CFO, human resources, or legal counsel).

4. Forecast the consequences.

5. Check the proposed decisions against values, goals, and mission.

6. Decide, determine, settle, conclude, and resolve. Decide on the best course of action; understand the probable result of the decision; settle any ancillary issues; conclude the process; and be resolved that the process has yielded the *best* course of action for the present.

NSBA (2006) also address common pitfalls leading to poor decision making.

- Framing the wrong question
- Not deliberating long enough before settling on a course of action
- Proceeding on poor information
- Acting under pressure
- Letting emotions get out of hand, or letting emotions drive decisions
- Failing to consider consequences
- Failing to admit mistakes or adjust to changing circumstances

This model represents excellent instruction and advice for school board members regarding a responsible approach to decision making. However, in this chapter, we will attempt to summarize a decision-making process and responsibilities that both support the NSBA summary and provide a practical application of decision making for superintendents and school boards. We will discuss a data-driven decision-making process, touching on issues of who collects and disseminates data and how subsequent decisions are made. We will then consider special issues that may arise during decision making, including lack of consensus, the authority behind decisions, consequences, and what happens when the team makes the wrong decision. Finally, we will discuss the impact of morality in decision making.

Data-Driven Decision Making

A commitment to decision making that includes copious and accurate data helps complete the first two steps of NSBA's decision-making model: (1) define the problem, and (2) gather information. Data-driven decision making is not a new term in the literature. It implies there is a reason or multiple reasons, which concrete information supports, that make one course of action more sensible to pursue over another. Data-supported decisions ultimately make the decision-making process easier because they provide concrete reasons behind difficult choices. Additionally, data-supported decisions confidently enforce board member decisions that oppose the popular but uninformed or misinformed opinions the public expresses.

Making decisions without supporting data is not only risky, it is completely irresponsible according to educational governance expectations. Data not only validate appropriate decisions, they protect decision makers from criticisms of their decision-making process. That is the important benefit of data: they are objective, and there are rarely multiple interpretations of indisputable facts.

For a board that is largely represented by veteran members, these data requirements can seem to be overkill. They may believe they know, from experience, the right course of action in a circumstance—and that may be the case. However, their decision-making comfort, emanating from experience, can lull them and their superintendent into a false sense of security. Even if both are right, they must be prepared to justify both the recommendation and the decision. Simply stating "That's the way we have always done things!" is not a sufficient reason; there must be readily available data supporting administrative recommendations and subsequent school board decisions. Plus, if some members have fewer than two years on the board, the absence of data prior to a decision can appear confusing or irresponsible and imply that new board members are encouraged to make decisions in the absense of data.

Data-driven decisions raise three questions.

1. Who gathers the data?
2. How are data disseminated?
3. How are decisions made?

Who Gathers the Data?

Providing thorough and objective data to support recommendations and ultimate decisions for authorizing an allocation of resources is the superintendent's primary responsibility. This is one of the ways that the superintendent, as the district CEO, continually verifies to the school board why it chose him or her to lead its district. Although information delivered to support a recommendation may be a function of delegation, the ultimate accountability for every recommendation and its supporting data resides in intraschool board–superintendent communications.

Board members can and should contribute freely to the process of data gathering prior to the board formally voting on a recommendation. However, unless the board authorizes the member to gather specific data on its behalf, the member should not presume to operate on behalf of the board; individual board members are not the school district's designated information gatherers. Board members can contribute when their personal knowledge of a circumstance, or experience in a situation or regarding a topic, lends insight that is beneficial to an administrative recommendation or board decision. However, if the administration is charged with the responsibility to bring back a recommendation and a board member does not have specific information pertinent to the recommendation, board members should rely on their administrators to provide what has been requested of them and not pursue independent action mirroring what the administration has been charged to provide.

School board members can and should participate in the sharing of data. The recommended methods for sharing data with the school board–superintendent team will be discussed in the section How Are Data Disseminated?. More and more school boards and superintendents are taking advantage of working sessions in between regular business meetings to review and fully discuss data and supporting documentation for potential recommendations of future agenda items. This is an excellent opportunity to present the data, discuss potential pitfalls, identify areas where additional information is necessary, and so on. It is also an ideal setting for board members to express their personal positions or to present information they believe is germane to future decisions.

How Are Data Disseminated?

The agenda packet—information supplied to school board members in advance of a school board meeting—is a vital communication tool for superintendents and board members. School board members rely on this premeeting information to prepare for public meetings where they conduct the business of the corporation and respond to administrative requests for administration recommendations. These packets, whether delivered as hard copies or electronically, are important preparatory materials for school board members to review. The material not only informs, but also enables board members to formulate questions to challenge and clarify their superintendent's position on specific items requiring board consideration, formal action, or both. It is at this stage that steps three through five of the NSBA's (2006) model occur: get the superintendent's recommendation and consider alternatives; forecast consequences; and check proposed decisions against the organization's values, goals, and mission.

Typically, an agenda packet should be delivered for board consideration no less than two business days before a meeting where the board is expected to act on a specific recommendation. Board members should review administrative recommendations with their supporting data and internally either accept, reject, or frame questions for the superintendent on the recommendations when they receive the packet. That review should happen the same day the packet is distributed to the board.

If there are questions about the supporting material, the recommendation itself, or how to interpret the data, the board member should contact the superintendent or his or her designee the day following the distribution of the agenda packet and supporting documentation to the school board. Waiting to criticize information or ask for additional information at the board meeting where the superintendent is expecting the board to make decisions is irresponsible. It defeats the purpose of the board agenda packet, constitutes a surprise element, and elevates distrust within the school board–superintendent team. Additionally, waiting until the meeting night arrives to share concerns, questions, or opinions, when a decision is expected to occur is not only a bane on school board governance, it potentially delays important decisions unnecessarily. If a board member may discover data that contradicts data that a superintendent is using to advance a recommendation for formal approval, it is important for the board member to share the data. However, the member's motive should not be divisive, critical, or accusatory of the administration when sharing those data; rather, the goal should be to share information that the superintendent may not have been aware of. Only under rare occasions would this type of information sharing occur in a public meeting. Most often it would be shared in a working session prior to a public meeting where discussion and a vote on a recommendation would normally occur.

How Are Decisions Made?

The final step of the NSBA's (2006) decision-making model—*Decide, determine, settle, conclude, and resolve*—relates to making the actual decision. Frequently, informal decisions are reached by compromise and consensus. These terms are often misunderstood as synonymous; however, *compromise* and *consensus* represent different thought processes and convey different attitudes in decision making and should not be used interchangeably.

Most people are familiar with the term *compromise*. Yet, few acknowledge that compromise represents a lose-lose scenario in any decision-making process. Compromise essentially means that both sides agree to forfeit something to reach agreement; neither side gets everything it wishes. Although compromise is a common tactic and well-known strategy in collective bargaining negotiations, it is a lesser-desired method in decision making. It makes it too easy to settle for what can be than strive for what ought to be, and it leaves both sides feeling short-changed.

Consensus is much more preferable for a school board–superintendent team. *Consensus* is often incorrectly used to mean the majority of stakeholders' opinion. Decision making according to this strategy—deciding via *majority opinion*—often resonates with board members and superintendents because it allows for a quick decision to be made in favor of those who hold the most common opinion in spite of internal disagreements about a recommendation. However, a true *consensus* actually means that one or more members are not decided on their official position, but are not sufficiently opinionated on the matter to take a stand on the recommendation under consideration. In effect, they can abstain from a voting decision. The fact that a member or members are not decided is important because reaching a consensus only works when "there is substantive agreement in principle among the group, and, more importantly, it works when there is an *informed* lack of agreement *plus* a genuine collective in achieving such agreement" (Pollard, 2011). An example of compromise is commonly seen in contract negotiations when school districts concede to a demand from a bargaining unit (for example, state teachers' associations, the American Federation of Teachers [AFT], or the American Federation of Labor and Congress of Industrial Organizations [AFL-CIO]) in exchange for something (hours worked or fringe benefit concessions) wanted by the school district administration. On the other hand, consensus means that both sides realize there is an issue, but are willing to work to find a solution that is mutually beneficial without compromise. Although school board decisions are determined by a simple majority, that decision can represent consensus, since board decisions are representative of board position.

Although the decision-making process can seem straightforward, there are certain issues that may arise during the process that will potentially hamper the school board–superintendent team's efficacy. This chapter will now discuss some special considerations in decision making and how teams can overcome these issues.

Special Considerations in Decision Making

Many issues may affect a team's effort to make a firm and effective decision. In this section, we will consider four of the most common issues: (1) when the decision is not unanimous, (2) when the decision is not for the board, (3) when decision making has consequences, and (4) when the team makes the wrong decision.

The Decision Is Not Unanimous

It is possible that some issues presented to a school board–superintendent team, despite the best information available, will lead to different opinions regarding courses of action. That is the beauty of the governing system school districts have under local school boards. Member diversity helps to ensure that the board reaches the best decisions by approaching each issue and interpretation of data from different backgrounds and life experiences.

Not every decision needs to be unanimous, and there is no requirement that any be unanimous. Split decisions are an ordinary reality of board member service, and if the board is split on decisions from time to time, that is to be expected. After all, if everyone thought alike, there would only need to be one member on the board. However, it is important to acknowledge that if the board is continually split, it could be a sign of a greater dysfunction, especially if split decisions seem to result from subjective interpretations of objective data.

It is important for board members and superintendents to gain a working knowledge of each other—both for the superintendent to understand board member dynamics and personalities and also for the board to understand its own makeup. Life experiences, personalities, and individual decision making are inextricably linked. Understanding what drives individual positions on particular issues is insightful for everyone on the school board–superintendent team, both for avoiding sensitive issues, as well as anticipated support for proposals. This is where the importance of professional development applies. Understanding board decision making, data interpretation, board dynamics, and community relations in decision making is a daunting task. This is especially true for new board members, but if veteran board members are true to themselves, they wrestle with the same issues. The responsibility of making decisions is weighty, but having trust in one's team members can allow decision making to proceed without undue difficulty.

The Decision Is Not for the Board

In chapter 3 (page 35), we discussed *who does what*. Every school board must acknowledge that its responsibility is not to run the school. That job, by assignment or through delegation, is the superintendent's responsibility. The superintendent manages these multimillion-dollar public education institutions on a day-to-day basis and must have the latitude to do so. If a superintendent had to wait on board approval for every decision that needed to be made in between board meetings, the school district would be in disarray. This is where policy and job descriptions enter the decision-making equation.

A superintendent does not need to wait for school board authorization when he or she is given the authority to act in a particular circumstance or in compliance to a specific requirement. The superintendent is CEO of a public school district, and thus is vested with all the decision-making authority that state and local policy designates to his or her position. However, it does not negate the requirement to provide the data that support his or her action in accordance with existing statute or local policy. Neither does it supplant the superintendent's need to communicate his or action actions to the board. Boards should ensure that any decisions that are appropriate for a superintendent should be passed along to the person responsible for the relevant consequences.

The Decision Has Consequences

School boards are elected to conduct business. Whatever else may accompany election jargon, and whatever reasons candidates state for wanting to be a school board member, the bottom line is that a board member must be prepared to participate in the district's governance. It goes without saying that making decisions is an important part of a board member's governance responsibility. Although not every decision will require an in-depth investigation or a review of multiple alternatives, every decision is important, and board members need to understand the potential impact of their decisions before a vote occurs.

Each decision the school board–superintendent team makes is an opportunity to engender trust with each other and with the public. Trust that is earned is never taken for granted or taken at face value; it is always supported by honest intent, responsible actions, and unwavering institutional accountability. Making the best recommendations, supported by sound reasons, and a willingness to stand behind the recommendation is the type of executive leadership school boards desire and 21st century educational governance climate demands.

The Team Makes the Wrong Decision

It is important to acknowledge that the most current decision-making processes, the most up-to-date information, and the best of intentions will not guarantee that every decision will ultimately be the *right* one; for this reason, this last thought on decision making is worth consideration. If we accept that no school board–superintendent team member is infallible and that collectively a decision it makes may ultimately prove to be a mistake, the worst thing is to cover it up, pretend it did not happen, or redirect the responsibility to someone else. Instead, follow these three simple steps.

1. **Understand it:** Make sure you understand what current data are providing that contradicts the board's previous action.

2. **Own it:** Accept that the previous decision, however well intended, was incorrect or is no longer viable.

3. **Correct it:** Proceed with the corrective action that provides the *best* solution after consideration of the latest information.

Hindsight will always be 20/20, while anticipating what the results of every decision might be is never an exact science. If a decision needs to be modified or reversed, the school board–superintendent team is well advised to remember that the courage to admit a mistake is an important part of leadership and establishing credibility with school district stakeholders. Addressing errors responsibly does not mean that there will not be some measure of fallout over a decision that is subsequently found questionable, but it does mean that the team is not only determined to make decisions, it is determined to make the right and best decisions possible.

Professional Development Activity on Decision Making

This activity helps teams practice consensus building and speaking with a unified voice regarding an issue or proposed decision. It allows teams to practice situations in which a decision is not unanimous, but a unified response is still required.

Time Frame

This activity takes thirty to sixty minutes to complete.

Materials

The team will need a facilitator, flip chart paper and markers, and a copy of the *fist to five* strategy (see figure 5.1). A good facilitator is integral to this activity. The facilitator should be artful in identifying common areas of agreement and summarizing statements for the group.

Five fingers: I love this proposal. I will champion it.

Four fingers: I strongly agree with the proposal.

Three fingers: The proposal is okay with me. I am willing to go along.

Two fingers: I have reservations and am not yet ready to support this proposal.

One finger: I am opposed to this proposal.

Fist: If I had the authority, I would veto this proposal, regardless of the will of the group.

Source: DuFour, DuFour, Eaker, Many, & Mattos, 2016.

Figure 5.1: *Fist to five* strategy.

*Visit **go.SolutionTree.com/leadership** to download a free reproducible version of this figure.*

Process

The team should do the following.

1. As a team, decide on an issue or proposed decision that may have divided opinions among team members. Post the issue or proposed decision on flip chart paper.

2. Discuss the *fist to five* strategy (DuFour, DuFour, Eaker, Many, & Mattos, 2016) using the chart in figure 5.1 (page 67). Have this visual available during the activity. Note: If team members would prefer to not use the *fist to five* gestures, the facilitator can simply call out the number or response (for example, Who would *never* support this issue or decision? Who *absolutely* supports this issue or decision?) and record the responses.

3. The facilitator now presents the issue or decision, and team members use the hand configurations to express their decision on the issue.

4. The facilitator records individual team member responses.

5. The facilitator now asks those members making a fist or holding one or two fingers to discuss why they rated the issue or decision at these levels. As they discuss those reasons, the facilitator writes the explanation or explanations on flip chart paper. If another member has a similar reason, the facilitator draws a check mark by the first reason.

6. This process is now repeated for members offering a rating of three, four, and five. Again, responses are recorded on flip chart paper and check marks used for repeated reasons.

7. The facilitator now asks team members responding with a fist or one or two fingers if they would be more comfortable supporting the issue or proposed decision if it was rewritten to include their concerns.

8. If these team members respond "yes," a rewritten issue statement or proposed decision is drafted, and the process is repeated for the new draft. The facilitator offers additional drafts if necessary to address concerns until the team members reach consensus.

While this activity was designed for a positive outcome, there will be times when a unanimous decision is not possible. In those cases, consider the following strategies.

- **Table the issue or proposed decision:** Reschedule the vote after allowing ample time to reconsider all sides of the issue or proposed decision. In some cases, alliances may form within the team during this down time and facilitate agreement.

- **Assess the level of trust among team members:** Oftentimes, lack of trust underscores the failure to reach agreement. It may be that the issue or proposed decision is set aside while the team addresses issues of trust. Specifically, team members must trust that the collective team's wisdom is greater than any one individual's.

- **Assess whether there are any hidden or unresolved issues:** A team member may have hidden or unresolved issues preventing him or her from supporting the proposal. If so, stop consensus building and address them.

- **Assign the latest draft of the issue or proposed decision to a smaller group within the team:** Have the smaller group bring a modified version back to the team for consideration.

- **Assess the tone of the consensus meeting:** Are members good listeners, solution centered, patient, nonjudgmental, and humble? If not, address these issues before consensus building moves forward.

- **Respect individual members' wishes:** It may be that a team member simply cannot support the proposed decision because it is counter to his or her beliefs or values. In this case, the team could respect the individual member's beliefs or values and support his or her voting "no" or abstaining from the vote.

Results

After participating in this activity, boards should emerge with a greater understanding of the differing moralities and decision-making styles within the group and the ways to counter these in the future.

Morality's Importance in Decision Making

When a school board makes a decision, every board member's voice counts equally, regardless of the experience he or she brings to the table. A sad truth of school board functionality is that, unfortunately, experience may not always be present to ground every decision made in a boardroom. This becomes evident when examining school board member turnover. In the authors' home state of Indiana, approximately 46 percent of the state's school board members only serve one four-year term (Indiana School Boards Association, 2015). That suggests that approximately 23 percent of Indiana's first-term school board members are elected every two years, representing a tremendous turnover in leadership, but one that is not unusual for school boards, as research shows elsewhere (Rice, 2014). Naturally, important decisions cannot wait until new board members gain sufficient experience on every issue that may arise between the time they take office and the point at which they meet the qualification as *experienced* enough to make a conscientious and responsible decision on a matter. However, it is this relatively high turnover rate and the resulting absence of experience that emphasizes the need for an innate sense of morality to be present in board members at the time of their election to the board—so that if decisions cannot be guided by experience, they can at least be guided by morality.

Dean Turner, a local farmer and long-time board member who had elected not to seek another term, gave Michael the following advice during Michael's first term. He stated, "Mike, you just need to make sure you use plain ol' horse sense," or what we now refer to as *common sense* (D. Turner, personal communication, April 5, 1974). Simply measuring decision making from a moral and personal sense of right and wrong does not suffice in every instance; however, it is an excellent starting point, and Dean was right on the mark with his advice. Having a good understanding of the culture and climate of community, combined with an understanding of the community's collective moral compass, provides a solid foundation in any decision-making process, especially if one falls short on experience. What will improve decisions in an environment of low experience and high turnover is a careful selection of board members and superintendents with excellent horse sense. Stakeholders can then feel confident that decisions are being made by trustworthy individuals with their best interests at heart.

Summary

Decision making is a huge part of a board member's responsibility, and one can argue that making decisions is predominantly why board members are essential to the public education governance model. Likewise, superintendents, as school districts' practicing CEOs, are crucial to the decision-making process. They provide information, guidance, and recommendations to school board members so they can make informed decisions on the operational matters and educational issues facing U.S. schools. All decisions should be grounded in objective data so that they can be justified to a skeptical public.

Providing and sharing data, communicating recommendations, asking questions, getting clarification, and anticipating the results of decisions before they are made are each important pieces of the decision-making process, and when employed objectively and thoughtfully these actions represent the combined leadership, management, and governance oversight strengths of the school board–superintendent team.

Chapter 6

Committed and Effective Team Leadership

Considering that a school board–superintendent team already exists in every school district, a key question for any team becomes, Is the team committed and effective? The word *team* is frequently referred to in leadership and governance. Whether it is *working as a team*, *building a team*, or *taking one for the team*, teams contribute to overall district operations, having the potential to support organizational success or serve as an organizational saboteur. This chapter will provide an overview of effective and committed team elements with implementation strategies.

Much research has centered on the topic of teams. Significant investigations began around the topic of groups as early as the 1930s, culminating in Kurt Lewin's (1944) concept of force field analysis identifying forces that helped and hindered groups. Kaushik Kundu and Debdas Ganguly (2014) move from the concept of a *group* to defining *team* as a collection of individuals relying on a collaborative approach for its joint responsibility of reaching goals. The authors' focus on the concept of "individuals collaborating to achieve goals" (Kundu & Ganguly, 2014, p. 28) forms the essence of the school board–superintendent team. Much theory and emergent thought contributes to a growing body of knowledge regarding teams; however, three factors most always determine team commitment and effectiveness: (1) effective team leadership, (2) strong relationships, and (3) insightful questions. The chapter will then discuss some implementation strategies teams can use to become a more committed and effective team.

Effective Team Leadership

Thinking of the school board–superintendent team over a period of time, leadership for the team may be fluid; the superintendent, board president, or another appointed team member may provide it depending on the context of the team's work and the goals to be accomplished. The team leader has a challenging and competing role in that he or she must lead the team while also being a team member. Consequently, staying engaged and participating in team membership, while also providing leadership, becomes an effectiveness imperative. If practiced consistently, the individual team member personalities begin to merge and a singular team consciousness emerges. At that point it may seem as if the team is the leader, rather than any one individual. Interestingly, Isaac Prilleltensky (2000) articulates this complex melding into a team consciousness as a form of leadership recognized as values-based, in which "personal interests and degrees of power held by people" give way to the team's cogent values (p. 141).

Regardless of who may be providing team leadership, certain traits and characteristics should be common among team leaders. Sherrie Scott (n.d.) finds that "compassion and integrity . . . inspire the trust and respect of the team." Ultimately, trust and leadership must go hand in hand. In the absence of trust, team leadership proves ineffective with a frequent overreliance on position power (such as "In my role as superintendent I have no choice but to support this agenda"), fear (for example, "The board must approve this, or we'll be sued for sure"), or both. Scott (n.d.) notes the following ten qualities of an effective team leader. Understanding these qualities through the school board–superintendent team lens provides greater insight into the team's leadership needs.

1. **Communication:** Clear and quality one-way (such as flyers) or two-way (such as discussion) communications from leaders helps ensure understanding and participation among team members. An emphasis on two-way communiques allows team leaders to invite input and listen to team members.

2. **Organization:** Sound organizational skills allow a systems approach to maintaining order and guiding team members toward district goals and objectives. Being organized moves beyond an ad hoc approach to accomplishing goals and objectives and builds predictability into how the team accomplishes things. This is especially important when the team meets publicly only once or twice per month.

3. **Confidence:** Leaders who are confident in their own decision making can be open to and inspire confidence in other team members' abilities, minimizing self-doubt and supporting clearer roles and responsibilities for all team members. A lack of confidence often yields team outcomes that are not sustainable or fully informed, creating a perception that the team is not committed to its decisions, frequently changes its mind, or makes poor decisions with little buy-in from district stakeholders. However, this should not be confused with the desirable quality of flexibility. Even the most

effective team leader realizes the complexity of schools and school districts and knows the team should be flexible enough to change when necessary.

4. **Respect:** Effective team leaders respect each team member's input and opinions. Simply stated, respectful team leaders value every voice. Offering respect also inspires respect in other team members and models an essential quality for other stakeholders in the district.

5. **Fairness:** Leaders must be consistent in their treatment of team members. Being *equal* is considered treating everyone the same, but is not as effective as *fair* treatment, which has more to do with consistent balance. Each team member is very different (for instance, experience, gender, race and ethnicity, professional background, and so on), and that difference should be embraced through fairness. Supporting fairness allows for the freedom of expression and ample interaction among team members.

6. **Integrity:** Leaders with integrity are considered honest and open. Leaders with integrity generally establish high trust among team members and are known as the leader who treats others as he or she would like to be treated.

7. **Influence:** Leaders with influence can inspire other team members' commitment and confidence. This characteristic is essential to managing a change agenda and inspiring action from the team.

8. **Delegation:** Through delegation, leaders get power by giving away power. Broader ownership of the team's agenda by team members deepens commitment and encourages individual participation. This compels the effective leader to know and understand each team member's strengths and challenges to help the team member realizes his or her potential.

9. **Facilitation:** As a facilitator, effective leaders help others understand and participate in the agenda to meet goals and objectives. Strong facilitation enhances participation by making it safe to take risks, be truthful, and speak up knowing all views will be considered.

10. **Negotiation:** Effective team leaders negotiate to achieve results, reach understanding, and solve problems in the best interests of all. Anticipating the diverse viewpoints, needs, and aims of team members, effective leaders seek common ground to reach agreements and resolve conflict inherent to teamwork.

Considering the preceding list of effective team leader characteristics, any leader possessing all ten qualities is often considered *visionary*: a leader who translates ideas into sustainable actions that best serve the school district's stakeholders. Yet, leadership alone does not make for an effective and committed team. The power of relationships must also be considered and understood, or team leadership quickly becomes a lonely proposition.

Strong Relationships

No matter what a person's role on the team may be, effective relationships are a cornerstone of team effectiveness. Human resources expert Susan Heathfield's (2015) work, which identifies seven actions to build relationships, defines the basis for effective team relationships.

1. **Offer solutions, not just problems, when the team meets:** Identifying problems is the easy part, but having solutions for the problems proves much more challenging. Solution-based conversations earn respect and admiration from the team. Be certain conversations are focused on problems and solutions, not the personalities often associated with the problems or solutions.

2. **Do not blame others:** Publicly and privately blaming others for team failures or shortcomings will erode relationships and invite anger and harsh criticism. When problems exist, deal with the source, not others.

3. **Pay attention to your communication:** Avoid any misunderstandings by refraining from sarcasm, anger, disrespect, or dubious joking in your verbal and nonverbal communications.

4. **Never blindside team members:** Operate from a no-surprises perspective. Blindsiding occurs when a team member hears about something involving them not from the team leader but instead in a public setting, such as a board meeting, or through others not directly involved in the particular issue. Whether this *gotcha!* moment was intentional or not, it erodes trust quickly.

5. **Honor commitments:** The work of governance and district leadership is very interconnected. Missing deadlines and commitments breaks down team effectiveness, strains relationships, and affects the work of many others relying on the team. It's important for team members to follow through and do what they say they will do!

6. **Share credit for completed work:** Rarely does one member accomplish all the team's work. Take time to promote the contributions of all those who helped and express appreciation for those that help you. A thank-you, reward, form of praise, or type of recognition should be handled publicly or privately, depending on individual team members. There is no

one-size-fits-all way to share credit. Knowing what motivates individual team members will guide the sharing of credit.

7. **Help others reach their potential:** Each team member has individual strengths and talents that define and distinguish him or her. Help each one harness that greatness to maximize his or her potential. Some may have finance expertise, while others are expert in strategic planning. Know each other well and exploit individual team member talents and skills.

When a team member embraces these seven actions, he or she is often referred to as a true *people person*: someone who truly cares. Clearly the school board–superintendent team survives in a climate of strain and challenge, yet the relational component of the team cannot be understated. Focusing on team member relationships yields enormous dividends by creating great teams in terms of commitment and effectiveness.

Insightful Questions

It has long been known that great teams ask great questions, with a deep commitment to listening more than speaking. Teams that ask questions grow and learn together, and researchers and scholars who devote their professional lives to the importance of asking questions support this important team investment to grow and learn. Psychologists and childhood learning experts Irving Sigel and Ruth Saunders (1977) wisely note that "question-asking promotes thinking [and] is a social good" (p. 2). In fact, former Google CEO Eric Schmidt says, "We run this company on questions, not answers" (as cited in Verstraete, 2014). Great questions make problems solvable and encourage collaboration. For an effective team to work with each other as well as other stakeholder groups associated with the school district, Verstraete (2014) suggests the following question prompts:

- Could you say more about . . . ?
- What are your main concerns?
- How might we mitigate those concerns?
- What would be the ideal outcome?
- What other options do you think we have?
- How can we best support you?
- How could we best work together collaboratively?

With a grounding in the concepts that underlie great leadership, team relationships, and the need to ask questions, teams are now prepared to practice their leadership skills in professional development activities.

Professional Development Activity on Leadership

This activity develops teams' questioning and listening skills and creates an environment of truthful disclosure. It allows teams to build on the power of questioning to bring the team closer together.

Time Frame

This exercise should take approximately thirty minutes.

Materials

This exercise calls for a facilitator, a recorder, a chalkboard or whiteboard (or other publicly viewable screen), chalk or markers, pens or pencils, and paper.

Process

After identifying a facilitator and a recorder, consider the following.

1. The group reviews the following eight questions as a team. It plans to respond to the first and second questions, and one additional question of its own choice, as a team. Note that the team can select as many questions as it would like but should allow for ten to fifteen additional minutes per question. The recorder should list responses from team members on a chalkboard, whiteboard, or other publicly viewable screen.

    a. Why did you run for the school board? or Why did you become an administrator?

    b. Think of an effective team you have worked with. What made it effective?

    c. What is your biggest hope for the board–administrative team?

    d. How do you learn best?

    e. What will you need to be the best board–administrative team member?

    f. What are two great things or points of pride about your district?

    g. What are the most important issues facing the board–administrative team?

    h. What might cause the board–administrative team to not accomplish its vision, mission, or both?

2. Each team member takes five minutes to individually respond to the questions, noting responses he or she would be comfortable sharing with the entire team.

3. The team facilitator should now bring the team back together and invite responses to the first question, "Why did you run for the school board?" or "Why did you become an administrator?" Open dialogue should guide the responses. The facilitator may want to ask questions for clarity, but should not judge the responses. For example, if someone states, "I did this because I care about kids in our community," a follow-up question might be, "What about your service to the board did you hope would benefit kids in our community?" The goal is to better understand why members committed to governance or administration.

4. The team facilitator now addresses the second and third questions individually, using a similar format for sharing among team members as with the first question. The recorder should list responses to the second and third questions so that the collection of responses is viewable to all. Regarding the second question ("Think of an effective team you have worked with. What made it effective?"), discuss the combined responses in terms of how they align with the team's current work. Consider the following clarifying questions—

    ◆ Is the brainstormed list of best-practice ideas already being used for our team?

    ◆ Were there any ideas we should consider adopting?

    ◆ Is there anything about our team that might be considered ineffective? Would any of the brainstormed ideas improve the ineffective aspects?

5. Conclude the activity by asking if there is anything else to discuss about the overall questions and responses that team members did not have the opportunity to share.

6. The facilitator, at his or her earliest convenience, should type and distribute the suggestions about best-practice ideas that were considered for adoption. This will serve as an important reminder of the commitments that can be easily utilized to strengthen team effectiveness.

Results

Participating in this activity hones questioning and listening skills and creates a climate of truthful disclosure. These benefits serve to bring the team closer together with agreed-on best-practice ideas.

Implementation Strategies

Thus far, this chapter has described the importance of team leadership, relationships, and the need to ask great questions. Thinking about these three broad areas affords ample opportunities to deepen team commitment and improve overall team effectiveness. However, teams should consider the following seven strategies to ensure implementation success.

1. Develop foundational statements.
2. Set goals.
3. Adopt a code of conduct and a code of ethics.
4. Set ground rules for meetings.
5. Define team member roles and responsibilities.
6. Move from congeniality to collegiality.
7. Pursue team growth through regular professional development and evaluation.

Develop Foundational Statements

The team should insist on a clear set of values or beliefs, mission, and vision statements. These foundational statements are described in great detail in chapter 7 (page 89); these statements provide a powerful venue to connect the team around what it believes most strongly about teaching and learning. Goal setting should be an outcome of the foundational statements.

Set Goals

Goals clarify the team's focus, effectively use time, focus decision-making priorities, and communicate the team's intentions to a variety of stakeholders. Goal setting may appear to be a straightforward and easy process; however, the challenge lies in prioritizing goals and reducing priority goals to a manageable number. Usually, five or fewer goals at the board–superintendent level is advisable. As goals are identified, a process to prioritize might include developing consensus through discussion, allowing team members to list their top five and select those with the greatest tally, or receive as much information about each goal and vote on a recommended set of goals.

Adopt a Code of Conduct and a Code of Ethics

Just as foundational statements and goals guide the team, a code of conduct and code of ethics can also assist in team leadership. The school board code of conduct establishes the basic rules of behavior for board members (see figure 6.1 for an example). On the other hand, the school board code of ethics focuses on principles that distinguish *right* and *wrong* (see figure 6.2, page 82, for an example). The American Association of School Administrators (n.d.) also has a code of ethics it promotes for superintendents (see figure 6.3, page 84), similar to its code of ethics for school board members. When distinguishing between the two codes, it helps to think of a code of ethics as principle focused and a code of conduct as rule focused. Both are essential to effective team functioning and may already be part of district policies. If so, reviewing and reaffirming them as a team is encouraged. However, if these are not part of current operation policy or practice, it is best to discuss and adopt these codes at a time when the school board–superintendent team is in a generally peaceful mode and not embroiled in any high-profile, controversial issues. Revising these codes in times of calm helps ensure successful implementation and can help refute claims or rumors that code adoption is a reactive action rather than a proactive one.

New Albany Floyd County School Board Compact

Conduct at a board meeting is very important. The school board desires to promote a legacy of a well-functioning, effective board. To facilitate that goal, we agree to avoid words and actions that create a negative impression on any individual, the board or the corporation. We will be open minded and willing to listen attentively to all speakers and presenters. We agree that we can disagree and will do so using common courtesy and respect for others. We will not react to impromptu complaints on the spot, but will assure that, after appropriate administrative investigation, legitimate concerns will receive the suitable attention of the administration.

The board agrees that it has one employee—the superintendent—and that the board and superintendent will work collaboratively to fulfill their mutually complementary roles in an atmosphere of trust combined with open and honest communication.

The board expects the staff, under the authority of the superintendent, to implement board policy; that means to develop the strategies and follow action plans formulated to accomplish the school corporation's educational goals and objectives. Respecting the staff's role and obligation to develop the means to achieve goals, the board will refrain from doing staff work and will not second-guess staff decisions that represent reasonable interpretations of board policy. The board recognizes that its purpose is to provide leadership through effective governance, but not through managerial oversight. As

---

Figure 6.1: Sample board code of conduct. continued →

such, the board acknowledges that its purpose is not to attempt to act in a managerial or supervisory capacity over other school corporation staff and that it will refrain from doing so.

A board member needs to be a skilled decision maker, but he or she must remember that decisions are to be made only by the board acting as a whole in an advertised public meeting. Individual opinions on matters being considered can and should be defended, but once a decision is reached, it should be accepted gracefully and implemented wholeheartedly. No individual school board member may unilaterally commit the whole board to a particular course of action.

The board hereby adopts the following working agreements and behavioral expectations as a minimum model of operation.

Working Agreements

Members operate under the following working agreements.

1. The board regards the creation of a vision and direction for the corporation to be a primary responsibility.

2. The board will not adopt any new program or service unless it aligns with and contributes to the school system's mission and vision.

3. The relationship between the superintendent and board members is collegial not hierarchical, based on mutual respect for their complementary roles.

4. The superintendent is accountable only to the full board of school trustees.

5. No board member or subset of the board of education has the authority to act or speak on behalf of the board without the board's consent.

6. The board and the superintendent have the right to expect performance and candor from one another.

7. Board members act in the best interest of all the students in the corporation.

8. Board members must respect the confidentiality of the executive session.

9. The board, both individually and as a whole, must accept responsibility for board processes and effectiveness.

10. Board members recognize that they have no individual authority, real or implied, except when duly the board authorizes them to act as its exclusive representative.

11. Board members will refrain from advising, supervising, or otherwise interfering with staff members during the performance of their responsibilities to the school corporation. Board involvement in staff decisions reduces the degree to which the staff can be held accountable and interferes with staff ownership.

12. Board members in the minority of a split decision will not sabotage the action; individuals on both sides of an issue will respect their board colleagues.

13. The board expects the superintendent to exercise his or her administrative authority to the fullest, bound, of course, by the parameters the board set in written board policy.

14. The board will clearly convey its leadership expectations to the superintendent, and will support its expectations through policies that enable the superintendent to implement the board's expectations through administrative procedures.

15. The board acknowledges that the superintendent is bound to honor only written board expectations.

16. The board will permit no fragmentation of its voice.

17. Board members may communicate with other individual members for purposes of asking questions, clarifying information, or socializing under circumstances that do not conflict with or circumvent the open-door law.

18. Board members may not communicate with other individual members for purposes of soliciting votes in support of or opposition to items of business that may come before the board.

19. The board president or designated members will serve as the board spokesperson to the media and members of the public on issues regarding board actions.

20. The superintendent or, in his or her absence, a specified designee, shall be the official corporation spokesperson to the media and members of the public on corporation issues.

21. Board members will refrain from independently engaging the media or audience in conversation without first seeking permission from the board president.

Behavioral Expectations

Each school board member will:

1. Respect our diverse community's needs and make decisions based on the common good for our students

2. Clearly identify issues and discuss them in an open, honest, and respectful manner

3. Seek to understand corporation issues in a broader perspective

4. Display personal integrity

5. Solve problems through a collaborative process where all participants support the decision and actively work toward its implementation

6. Acknowledge and celebrate the board's accomplishments with each other

7. Be respectful and genuinely concerned about the feelings of others

8. Create a safe environment for the productive exchange of ideas

continued →

9. Sincerely listen and seek to understand the viewpoints of others

10. Respect the expertise that others bring to the organization

Lastly, as advocates of public education and to model best practices in continuous improvement, the board expects member involvement in those professional development seminars and workshops designed to improve the board's governance effectiveness.

We hereby attest that we have read, understand and agree to adhere to this compact in the performance of the duties as a New Albany Floyd County Consolidated School Corporation school board member.

Board member: _____

Board member: _____

Board member: _____

Date: _____

Source: Adapted from New Albany Floyd County Consolidated School Corporation, 2010.

Indiana School Boards Association Code of Ethics

A school board member should honor the high responsibility that membership demands:

- By thinking always in terms of *children first*
- By understanding that the basic function of the school board member is *policymaking* and not *administrative*, and by accepting the responsibility of learning to distinguish between these two functions
- By accepting the responsibility, along with fellow board members, to assure that adequate facilities and resources are provided for the proper functioning of schools
- By refusing to play *politics* in either the traditional partisan, or in any petty sense
- By representing the entire school community at all times
- By accepting the responsibility of becoming well-informed concerning the duties of board members, and the proper function of public schools.
- By recognizing responsibility as a state official to seek the improvement of education throughout the state

A school board member should demonstrate respectful relationships with other members of the board:

- By recognizing that authority rests only with the board in official meetings and that the individual member has no legal status to bind the board outside of such meetings

- By recognizing the integrity of previous board members and the merit of their work
- By refusing to make statements or promises as to how he or she will vote on any matter, which should properly come before the board as a whole
- By making decisions only after all facts bearing on a question have been presented and discussed
- By respecting the opinion of others and by graciously conforming to the principle of *majority rule*
- By refusing to participate in irregular meetings that are not official and when all members do not have the opportunity to attend
- By working with fellow board members and the administration to fairly determine the present and future educational needs of the community

A school board member should maintain desirable relations with the superintendent of schools and other employees:

- By striving to procure the best professional leader available for the head administrative position
- By giving the superintendent full administrative authority for properly discharging the professional duties of the position and the responsibility to achieve acceptable results
- By acting only after consideration of the superintendent's recommendations on matters of school governance
- By having the superintendent present at all meetings of the board except when his or her contract and salary considerations are under review
- By respecting proper communication channels, referring all complaints to the proper administrative office and considering them only after failure of an administrative solution
- By providing adequate safeguards around the superintendent and other employees so that they can perform their responsibilities
- By presenting criticisms of an employee directly to the superintendent

A school board member should maintain a commitment community:

- By developing and adopting a mission and a vision statement for the school corporation
- By conducting all school business transactions openly
- By vigorously seeking adequate financial support for the schools
- By refusing to use the school board position for personal gain
- By refusing to discuss confidential board business anywhere other than when attending a properly advertised board meeting
- By earning the community's confidence that all is being done in the best interests of school children

Source: Adapted from Indiana School Boards Association, 2010.

Figure 6.2: Sample code of ethics.

AASA's Statement of Ethics for Educational Leaders

An educational leader's professional conduct must conform to an ethical code of behavior, and the code must set high standards for all educational leaders. The educational leader provides professional leadership across the district and also across the community. This responsibility requires the leader to maintain standards of exemplary professional conduct while recognizing that his or her actions will be viewed and appraised by the community, professional associates and students.

The educational leader acknowledges that he or she serves the schools and community by providing equal educational opportunities to each and every child. The work of the leader must emphasize accountability and results, increased student achievement, and high expectations for each and every student.

To these ends, the educational leader subscribes to the following statements of standards.

The educational leader:

1. Makes the education and well-being of students the fundamental value of all decision making

2. Fulfills all professional duties with honesty and integrity and always acts in a trustworthy and responsible manner

3. Supports the principle of due process and protects the civil and human rights of all individuals

4. Implements local, state, and national laws

5. Advises the school board and implements the board's policies and administrative rules and regulations

6. Pursues appropriate measures to correct those laws, policies, and regulations that are not consistent with sound educational goals or that are not in the best interest of children

7. Avoids using his or her position for personal gain through political, social, religious, economic, or other influences

8. Accepts academic degrees or professional certification only from accredited institutions

9. Maintains the standards and seeks to improve the effectiveness of the profession through research and continuing professional development

10. Honors all contracts until fulfillment, release, or dissolution mutually agreed on by all parties

11. Accepts responsibility and accountability for one's own actions and behaviors

12. Commits to serving others above self

Source: Adapted from AASA, n.d.

Figure 6.3: Sample superintendent code of ethics.

Set Ground Rules for Board Meetings

Additionally, teams should establish basic ground rules for board meetings. These, too, may be part of the district's policy and should be reviewed and reaffirmed. We, the authors, are often reminded of the power of basic ground rules when, as an example, school board–superintendent teams struggle with *public comment* versus *public discussion*. Addressing the team publicly is very different than talking with the team publicly. While teams may appropriately receive information publicly via a patron's comments, all reaction, discussion, question asking, brainstorming, and decision making should be reserved for a later time. Having such discussions at public board meetings consumes much meeting time, often leads to uninformed and hasty decisions, and may leave the team appearing ineffective when basic protocol is not used to resolve issues. Adhering to basic ground rules will minimize this challenge and many others.

Define Team Member Roles and Responsibilities

Teams should define member roles and responsibilities as clearly as possible. Chapter 4 (page 45) describes the complex relationship of role and responsibility overlap in much greater detail. The goal in focusing on roles and responsibilities is to create the right mix of skills, talents, and experience to guide the team toward its stated outcomes. It is noteworthy that roles and responsibilities may change as the scope and nature of the team's work changes. The team should resist one-size-fits-all models, in which the superintendent or board president, for example, always assumes the same role or responsibility. It is understood that slight role and responsibility changes may create tension, but effective teams deal with this tension and are able to predict it. Town hall meetings hold an example of flexible roles. Consider a town hall meeting that has been scheduled for a review of gifted and talented education. The anticipated audience is these students' parents. In this case, the school board–superintendent team may decide the superintendent is best served to facilitate the meeting given his or her strengths in curriculum and instruction for exceptional learners. However, if the topic for the town hall meeting regards facility improvement with an intended audience of community members, most having no children in school, an elected or appointed official may be the best facilitator given that he or she represents the community's constituency.

Move From Congeniality to Collegiality

When the team works together, it should move beyond congeniality (being friendly and pleasant) to being collegial (respecting each other's abilities to work toward a common purpose). It is one thing to greet a team member and take a personal interest in him or her or his or her family (for instance, congenial), and another thing to roll up one's sleeves and engage in the difficult work of solving problems on behalf of the district (for instance, collegial). The goal is to strive for both congeniality and collegiality, but never confuse one for the other. It is much easier to be congenial than collegial. The effective team always knows and cares about each other, but respects, values, and listens to one another as well.

Pursue Team Growth Through Regular Professional Development and Evaluation

Teams should pursue the strategy of team growth through professional development and evaluation on a regular basis. Professional development may be formal, such as dedicated closed sessions where the team has an opportunity to think deeply and make meaning of a particular topic. Formal opportunities might also include travel and participation at a conference together. Informal professional development may take the form of a standing agenda item at regular board meetings, such as a Spotlight on Excellence, in which a school presents to the team on a particular topic that is a point of pride. Whatever form of professional development is pursued, it should not be episodic (for instance, something we only think about when challenges arise or the need exists). Rather, it should be strategically planned at least one year at a time. Evaluation is also essential; see chapter 11 (page 137) for a discussion on it. Evaluation helps the team understand if it has become complacent in some areas or if new skills are needed to respond to the constant changes in education. Evaluation is an effective means of stepping away from day-to-day operations to address more fundamental issues. A variety of evaluative means are available, such as questionnaires, interviews, or both. Annual evaluation is advised.

These are just a few leadership and teamwork strategies teams may consider when seeking to establish themselves as effective school board–superintendent teams. When implemented together, these strategies should help a team deepen its relationships, improve its leadership skills, and increase its chances of success in governing the school district.

Summary

Findings conclude that strong leadership and healthy relationships underscored by trust and respect define effective and committed teams (Heathfield, 2015; Kundu & Ganguly, 2014; Lewin, 1944; Prilleltensky, 2000; Scott, n.d.; Sigel & Saunders, 1977). Additionally, great teams ask great questions and understand the art of listening. Building on these basic concepts, we suggested seven implementation strategies to ensure team effectiveness: (1) developing foundational statements, (2) goal setting, (3) adopting a code of conduct and a code of ethics, (4) setting ground rules for meetings, (5) defining team member roles and responsibilities, (6) moving from congeniality to collegiality, and (7) pursuing team growth through regular professional development and evaluation.

part ii

Strategic and Evaluative Functions of School Board– Superintendent Teams

Chapter 7
Foundational Statements

This chapter addresses *foundational statements*—those statements used to guide decision making and planning, while defining and providing purpose for the daily performance of every employee in the school district. These underpinning statements, which aim to strengthen the local fabric of education, equally bind even those individuals that only periodically brush against public education within the district. (Board members are good examples.) Many school districts have adopted these kinds of statements only to allow them to quietly expire on the walls of their buildings, at the top of their letterhead, and on their business cards, relatively unnoticed, never remembered, out of sight, and out of mind. For all practical purposes, in these instances, they are dead documents (Derbeko, 2014).

However, if we are to defend why these documents should remain viable, then there must be an answer to the purpose foundational statements serve. That is a crucial question and one that deserves answering before proceeding any further. Certainly, any serious suggestions are likely to meet resistance unless there are significant reasons to support these statements' value within the school district's governance and operational framework.

The reason foundational statements are important is because every organization that hopes to be successful and remain relevant—whether it be a school district, private business, non-profit, or otherwise—requires a mechanism that, when followed, ensures that everyone is working toward the same thing, at the same time, and for the same reasons. As one superintendent notes, these statements "serve as a reference to all employees . . . providing clarity as we focus on student-centered decision-making" (D. Deweese, personal communication, January 9, 2017). More will be clarified regarding this mechanism throughout the chapter as we examine the foundational categories of core values and belief statements, mission statements, and vision statements, and the importance of stakeholder buy-in.

Core Value and Belief Statements

Core value and belief statements represent what an organization esteems most highly, and more importantly, what it will not compromise. The fact is that all of us have many *good* values and beliefs regarding education in our local districts—enough that, if named, would result in a very long list. However, these statements can be misleading unless given careful thought. Although the values and beliefs we could list would undoubtedly be good, the truth is that under various circumstances, many of these good values and beliefs would likely be surrendered or set aside as the unfortunate victims of circumstance. Special programs, reduced class sizes, extracurricular and cocurricular activities, or other programs or activities that reside outside a commonly defined basic list of educational wants and needs are examples of outcomes based on good values. Very few, if any, of these school districts' discontinued services and programs would actually qualify as *bad*; they are just not *core*. Core values and beliefs are those that remain regardless of circumstance. One can gain much insight into the character of a school district, what is most important to that district, and what will likely remain in that district when everything else fails when one considers a list of a district's core values and beliefs.

It is often during the discussion regarding core values and beliefs that the district's culture and climate emerges. Of course, many school districts identify a number of core values and beliefs that are common between them. This is not surprising given that common political statutes and shared public expectations for education bind each. However, they often emphasize other values and beliefs that emanate from and are representative of local expectations, traditional backgrounds, or both—providing a distinctive perspective. School districts commonly reflect the characters of the communities where they are located and this makes every district similar, but uniquely different.

An overlooked benefit of core values and beliefs is that, when thoughtfully adopted, they represent criteria for employment. As such, they are valuable tools in the new employee interview process. This is because these foundational statements are not optional tenets, or ignored or casually cast-aside personal opinions, but standards representing key expectations of employees in the performance of their individual roles and responsibilities.

It is true that no mandate exists that will force an employee to internalize beliefs and values that he or she is not inclined to adopt. However, a reasonable expectation of school boards and superintendents is that, regardless of a district employee's personal objections, his or her performance should always reflect and support district values and beliefs. Consequently, any employee who in good conscience cannot or will not adopt or modify his or her behavior to support district values and beliefs in the performance of individual roles and responsibilities should expect an invitation to go elsewhere. Equally important is the oversight and administrative resolve that this invitation, whether swift or after due process, is not compromised. The school district should never endorse a person in its employment that cannot or will not follow the district's core values or core beliefs. They are not optional.

The following are examples of core value and belief statements.

- We believe all students can learn.

- We believe "student achievement and character development are shared responsibilities among students, parents, community, and all school employees" (Community Schools of Frankfort, n.d.).

- We value "differentiated instruction that reflects best practices and is aligned with curriculum and assessments" (Community Schools of Frankfort, n.d.).

- We value "integration of technology into instructional practices at all grade levels" (Community Schools of Frankfort, n.d.).

Mission Statement

Mission statements are often confused with vision statements (page 92), and vice versa, but the two are easily distinguishable by remembering that the mission statement only answers one question: *Why?* Why does everyone in the school district do what they do? The district's purpose is defined by *why* and represents an all-encompassing reason for being that envelops every position, from the boardroom to the boiler room. Answering the *why* question not only establishes the context of the conversation during development, but helps to ensure that the statement is more easily committed to memory. In other words, succinctly defining a statement of purpose that is broad enough to cover all employees in the district and short enough to make it easy for every employee to remember is the goal of mission development (OnStrategy, n.d.).

A question frequently arises inquiring whether each individual school within the same district should have a distinct mission statement. (Some accreditation agencies require this.) We believe this is unnecessary. In the grand scheme, it is difficult to understand how the purpose of an elementary school can be different from the one of the high school; likewise, the middle school or junior high from the elementary, and so on. Borrowing a mission statement from one Indiana school district makes this point. Their mission statement is, "Educating today's students for tomorrow's challenges" (School Town of Highland, n.d.). One superintendent notes that statements such as this "are a constant reminder to keep us focused on strategic initiatives"

(N. Wahl, personal communication, January 9, 2017). By reading Highland's statement of purpose, it would be difficult to say how its mission would not apply to every school in its district. Furthermore, as the whole district's statement of purpose, the intent is that every employee has an obligation to fulfill that mission within his or her individual job responsibilities.

This drives home another important consideration: while it is perhaps easy to understand how board members, superintendents, administrators, and teachers fit into a statement of purpose, it is more difficult to understand its relationship to auxiliary and support staff. However, these individuals are every district's education enablers. They assist teachers and administrators in the performance of their duties, transport students, feed them, help supervise them, and clean up after them. Truly, education would not exist as we know it without these individuals. Is their role the same as that of board members, superintendents, administrators, and teachers? Of course not. Nevertheless, should the district's mission still apply to these individuals? Absolutely it should! However, the real question is whether these individuals understand their equal accountability for supporting the district's mission and if they understand their role within the context of the statement of purpose. If not, then an excellent learning and team-building opportunity presents itself for administrators and supervisors to review the mission statement with these employees and to have a crucial conversation with them regarding how their roles, individually and in combination with other school employees, fulfills the school district's purpose.

After identifying what is most important, what will not be compromised, and developing the district's statement of purpose, the next question is to define where the district is going. The district's *vision statement* is the third category of foundational statements.

Vision Statement

Our definition of a vision statement is *the desirable future state of the organization*, or in our case, the school district. It is not a statement of *what is*, but rather *what can be* in a realistically imagined future (Smith, 2016). The term *realistic* is important, but it should not be confused with unimaginative or uninspiring. A realistic vision statement addresses a district's future from a reasonable perspective that, while challenging, is still attainable.

Great vision statements rely heavily on imagination, not only in their final view of the future, but also in planning and constructing the statement. One of the best ways to get an idea of what the school district's future might be is to go there—visit the future. We figuratively traverse time and space every time we allow ourselves to dream. Our imaginations take us far away from our present circumstances and enable us to experience different realities, all without ever leaving the room. That imaginative thinking process is where visions are born, and when tempered with sensible, pragmatic guidelines, the results can be nothing less than astonishing.

Teams should take a mental trip to the future—say five or ten years from now—and describe what they see. Teams shouldn't write their descriptions of what should be or could be; rather, describe what members see as if it already exists. From their imagination's vantage point, the future members have imagined already exists, so describe it that way. The types of things teams might look for are the state of facilities, the relationship between the district and the community, the characteristics of future graduates, and the sort of student achievement tenets that are stressed. The list could go on, because the future likely consists of many things that are simply not currently realized in public education. The following are vision statements two Indiana school corporations developed. From Community Schools of Frankfort (n.d.):

> The Community Schools of Frankfort is a place where students and parents choose to attend, and highly effective personnel desire to work. Students will be provided a rigorous and relevant curriculum that begins with early childhood education and extends beyond the classroom. Technology will be highly utilized across the curriculum, and students will apply their talents to impact their lives and the world around them. CSF faculty and staff will be supported through professional development and have access to state-of-the-art facilities and resources made possible through sound fiscal management. Achievement will be a shared responsibility among stakeholders, thus developing a sense of pride within the community.

From Maconaquah School Corporation (n.d.), "The vision of Maconaquah Schools is to be a premier educational institution and the heart of the community, where students develop all skills necessary to succeed within a collaborative learning environment that is safe, challenging, and innovative."

Having expressed a desire to develop foundational statements, the first consideration is to assemble a team of the right people to do the developing. Too often, superintendents and school boards prefer to work in a vacuum for efficiency purposes since gathering together for such activities is difficult, but in this instance, that approach represents an error of omission. Foundational statements, as stated earlier, are for school boards and school district employees; consequently, if these statements are for them, it stands to reason that these groups must also be represented in their development.

Representative participation is a crucial component to subsequent buy-in or endorsement for the finished product. Ideally, the superintendent, school board members, and the entire administrative team (minimally, central office administrators and building-level administrators) should comprise the group in this effort. An essential reason for including the administrative team is that it has the critical task of implementation and enforcement. School board members, while participating in developing and adopting these statements, thereby establishing their importance, are not in a position to implement or to enforce them; that is an administrative responsibility. Other key community and school district personnel can be included as well, at the superintendent and board's discretion, but every effort should be made to ensure that the group's size will support scheduling and communication during the process without compromising creativity, while representing a diverse array of key education stakeholders.

Stakeholder Buy-In

Once the vision statement is imagined, the foundational statement trilogy is complete, but the work has just begun. The important task of disseminating these statements throughout the district begins, but that begs the question, *Who are these statements for?* Undoubtedly, these statements are primarily for the school board, superintendents, administrators, teachers, and support staff. However, it is common to want to include students, parents, or the community (in general) in that list as well. Understandably, a district team wants those groups' endorsement, but it is important to acknowledge that these statements do not bind or guide those outside groups; rather, those outside groups are the beneficiaries of them. The real benefit for sharing the statements is to elicit community support, instill community pride, and to raise another level of community accountability that foundational statement expectations provide and encourage.

Certainly, if these statements have never been in place, or if they are replacing dead documents, introducing how and why these statements are important is imperative. It could be a huge culture shock if everyone in the school district, from the boardroom to the boiler room, is being told that he or she is now accountable to support and further the district's foundational statements. In those instances, simply developing and adopting foundational statements will do little, if anything, without the proper due diligence to instill them into the school district's culture and climate through day-to-day operations.

Identifying *who* is responsible to accomplish this task or what role everyone plays once the development activity is finished is paramount to successful implementation. The school board has an important role, but not from an administrative perspective. Rather, it is responsible for empowering administrators and other key personnel in the district through its expectation of implementing, observing, and utilizing foundational statements in its everyday activities, as well as for present and future planning and decision making. It is in these oversight and management roles that the board–administrative team functions effectively.

It is the school board's responsibility to establish this expectation, while simultaneously monitoring how effectively it is received and instilled throughout the district. However, the board's role is not one of implementation. Implementation is strictly an administrative function, beginning with the superintendent as the key driver. As the CEO, the school superintendent works through key administrators who, in turn, disseminate expectations, develop strategies and receive implementation updates, remove roadblocks, and so on.

The importance of foundational statements is easy to defend in current literature (Coleman, 2013; Kokemuller, n.d.), but simply developing and recognizing the importance of these statements does not automatically ensure a cooperative and visionary atmosphere throughout the district. Successfully implementing the beliefs within meaningful foundational statements begins by building habits that continually and objectively measure everyday decisions, ideas, and strategic initiatives against the district's beliefs and values, mission, and vision. The closer the alignment and support rendered to those guiding statements, the greater the probability that the decision, idea, or initiative under consideration is not only something that can be done or the right thing to pursue, but also that it represents the best use of resources. In the 21st century educational climate, resources are limited, so ensuring that they are being utilized for their best possible return on investment is essential.

Professional Development Activity on Developing Foundational Statements

This activity helps team members develop foundational statements for their school or district (assuming that none of these statements are already in place). If a school district already has some or all of its foundational statements in place, this activity allows teams to review their existing statements for possible inclusion in the new draft. Teams may use the activity as a way to discover their district's unique culture.

Time Frame

It is not uncommon for this activity to take a minimum of three or four sessions, with each session lasting two and a half to three hours. Even if activities are merely affirming the existing foundational statements, ample time should be provided to review and reflect on the overall discussion and dialogue. Remember to schedule the exercise at a time that ensures all participants can attend. Furthermore, try to have the sessions no more than two weeks apart. This helps ensure continuity and prevents any loss of task momentum, while preventing the exercise from turning into a never-ending workshop.

Materials

Teams need a facilitator, a chalkboard or whiteboard, markers, pens or pencils, and paper.

Process

There are several ways to conduct this activity, but engaging an outside consultant to facilitate the process is highly recommended. An outside facilitator can help remove mental roadblocks and keep everyone focused in each session. The state school board association is a good resource for these types of workshops, but there are a number of private consultants who are familiar with this type of activity as well.

When completing this task, remember that there is no set length for foundational statements, and that they may vary as needed for local district buy-in. For example, in some districts, longer vision statements may capture the essence of the district's dream and how it intends to accomplish it, which implicitly includes core values and beliefs. In other districts, the vision and mission statements simply do not express everything that is necessary, and core values and belief statements are essential to communicate all that is distinctive to the district. The process should begin with identifying core values and beliefs, then move to crafting mission and vision statements.

Core Values and Beliefs

Teams should identify their core values and beliefs by doing the following.

1. Every participant submits a list of value and belief statements before the first meeting (for example, "I believe the district's curriculum . . . ," or "I value the district's personnel because . . ."). Alternatively, the facilitator can create eight to ten value and belief prompts that team members would complete. They should contribute one value or belief statement reflecting categories such as curriculum, facilities, student achievement, community relations, personnel, extracurricular activities, finance, and so on.

2. The facilitator compiles a master list of every participant's statements anonymously by category and then prepares to distribute that list at the first meeting.

3. At the first meeting the entire group assesses each statement to determine whether it represents a core value or belief. They determine this by asking, "Does the statement express a belief or value highly esteemed by the district, that is also viewed as an uncompromising statement or belief?" If "yes," keep it; if "no," discard it.

    ◆ The group interaction in this exercise will likely be tentative or even uncomfortable at the beginning, since this exercise requires judging individual contributions.

- Consequently, it is important for the facilitator to stress that participants judge statements not on whether they are good or bad, or right or wrong, but rather by deciding what is most important.

- Some statements will need revising and perhaps combining with portions of other statements to form value and belief statements that are reflective of the group's understanding about education in the local district.

4. After reducing this list, the group develops the mission and vision statements (page 97 and page 98). There is no specific number of value or belief statements required, but each should be easily defended as core to the district—that it is held in the highest regard and/or that it will not be compromised. It is a great practice to quickly review the value and belief statements at the start of each session. This not only helps to ensure that everyone is completely satisfied with these statements, it also helps to ingrain them in the group members' minds. It is not uncommon that these statements continue to evolve as the group goes through the remaining workshops and in response to everyone's understanding and expectation of the values and beliefs he or she identifies as *core*.

Mission Statements

The next team task is developing the mission statement. The goal is to develop a short, concise statement of purpose. The mission statement should be easily committed to memory and should clearly express *why* everyone in the school district operates as he or she does daily.

1. The facilitator divides the group into small teams. None should have more than six people, and school board members should be divided as equally between the total number of teams as possible.

2. The facilitator asks each group to move to a separate breakout area to begin its discussion and development of a mission statement or mission statements to recommend to the whole group.

3. Once each small team is finished (usually after forty-five minutes to an hour), the facilitator brings the entire group back together and allows each team to share its statements. There may be a statement or two that are immediately preferred, or there may be a need to combine portions of two or more statements.

4. Invite questions from members who need clarity. Encourage complete understanding of the statement's intent. However, discourage judgmental questions or comments about the statement.

This activity is usually accomplished in one session, paving the way to the final workshop session for developing the vision statement.

Vision Statements

The goal of this session is to create a vision statement that enables each team member to visualize a future, realistic, version of the school district. A vision statement can be powerful, but it should never be overly positive or utopian. Optimism tempered with realism is always preferable.

The method for developing vision statements is the same as for developing mission statements (page 97). Using the same teams from the mission statements' portion, consider the following.

1. The facilitator charges each team to develop a narrative statement that defines the future state of the school district using the criteria of a vision statement discussed earlier in this chapter.

2. After forty-five minutes to an hour, the whole team reassembles and each small-group facilitator shares its vision statement. Since narrative vision statements are much longer than the mission statements, usually comprising a paragraph or two, it is helpful for the group to identify the components in each vision statement that are most meaningful.

3. End the day's session.

In a second session:

1. The facilitator helps the entire team create its overall vision statement by combining the most preferred or meaningful elements from the individual group-created statements. If one contribution is used as a baseline statement, the facilitator should then incorporate the best elements from other statements, making sure not to compromise the readability. The same process is used even if the team begins by taking statements from each small team and constructing an entirely new paragraph.

2. Once these statements are completed and the entire group is satisfied, the group should work together to develop working goals. The most meaningful working goals describe the necessary activities required to reach the desirable future state of the school district. Using the vision statement to identify goals helps ensure the district's pursuit of the right, best things, and responsibility allocating the limited resources of the school district must apply to this effort.

3. After identifying working goals, the administrative team and superintendent are responsible for taking these high-level goals and building strategies, action plans, and timetables for goal attainment.

4. The administrative team and superintendent devise a reporting mechanism and frequency for keeping the school board apprised of goal progress. The foundational statements can provide focus and help to ensure that everyone is in lockstep with each other as he or she sets about to engage in the right, best activities to bring that desirable future into reality.

5. Once the statements are completed, it is recommended that they be prominently displayed in each building throughout the district, as well as on the district's website and social media sites. Additionally, it is recommended that the mission statement be added to the district's letterhead. Keeping foundational statements readily visible is an important first step to building the district culture around these statements.

Results

Participation in this activity, even with multiple sessions, has the potential to pay huge dividends in the board, administrator, and administrative team relationship. Within this activity alone, there is a tremendous opportunity for a dialogue of what is most important to a school district as each small group within the team frames the perspective. In addition, it clarifies who bears the greater responsibility for goal attainment. School boards authorize and empower, and the administration delivers. However, the mutual respect for each other's role in this critical exercise does not alienate one from the other, but serves to strengthen the school board–superintendent team. Further, it emphasizes the reliance each has for the other. To ensure success there must be mutual respect, for neither can succeed completely without the other. Teams succeed *together*.

Summary

Foundational statements ensure that all board members are working toward the same thing, at the same time, and for the same reasons. Activities to define, develop, or revitalize foundational statements are often met with resistance from superintendents, administrative team members, and school board members alike. We agree that statements alone do nothing without a mutual commitment to utilize the statements of value, belief, purpose, and vision to define and guide how the leadership team is to engage in effective, responsible public school governance. When the team goals and objectives reflect tenets of these statements and actions to meet them, the statements are not only reinforced but become a driving force in the school district culture and climate.

Chapter 8

Continuous Improvement and Quality Assurance

Simply stated, continuous school improvement is the single means that most clearly defines the school district's effectiveness. It means paying attention to the quality of what the school board–superintendent team does in support of teaching and learning—a way of thinking and acting that is never satisfied with the status quo. Given the myriad of roles and responsibilities the school board–superintendent team assumes, it is no wonder that a focus on continuous school improvement can seem daunting. Improvement tasks are often relegated to school-level emphases that key education professionals, such as teachers and building administrators, dominate. As Kirst and Wirt (2009) aptly note, there is "suspicion about the inability of school boards to provide academic leadership" (p. 147). Their rationale focuses on *effective school* research, which emphasizes school-based initiatives and school-based stakeholders—an approach often leaving school boards and district administrators void of meaningful participation. As a result, school boards and district-level leaders are frequently absent from school reform initiatives, despite the enormous potential for the school board–superintendent team to make a systems-level contribution. This chapter will address the team's involvement in continuous improvement throughout the district and the unique contributions the team has to offer to support and strengthen quality assurance through internal and external review processes.

Building on the foundational statements' concepts of chapter 7 (page 89), which included a focus on the development and implementation of a district's core values and beliefs, mission, and vision commitments, the school board–superintendent team is well positioned to think systemically about continuous school improvement and engage in comprehensive strategic planning. In the case of both continuous school improvement and strategic planning initiatives, teams should consider a bounded systems approach when asking the question, "What is working and what is not?" —an approach in which all aspects of the system are addressed and implemented, not just those things the team considers doable or easiest to tackle. Addressing only those components of strategic planning or continuous school improvement that are easy to accomplish serves to marginalize long-term and sustained gains for the district. For example, if a system for improvement has eight elements of focus, no meaningful value for systems thinking, planning, and acting is gained if only three or four elements are addressed. Typically, strategic planning and continuous improvement are considered as bounded systems that must be fully addressed.

Comprehensive Continuous Improvement

Bounded systems are important because they are considered whole or complete systems. Bounded systems have been thoughtfully researched and piloted over a sustained period of time and have been proven effective with little to no gaps that would leave the school board–superintendent team wanting for more (Park, Hironaka, Carver, & Nordstrum, 2013). Most important, bounded systems are generally valid and reliable (AASA, 2002; Stosich, 2014). In the simplest of terms, a valid system is trustworthy and of high quality. Reliability, in part, means that schools in different times and places, and which have different needs, should experience similar results by implementing the system in totality. In other words, the system is dependable.

So, what contribution can the school board–superintendent team make to continuous improvement while leaving emphasis at the school level for implementing such initiatives? We maintain the important contribution is that of *systems thinking*.

Systems Thinking

Authors Katheryn Gemberling, Carl Smith, and Joseph Villani (2000) note, "A systems thinker understands that everything is connected to everything else" (p. 3). In other words, in a complex school district environment, all aspects of the organization are connected. The individual parts may comprise faculty, staff, students, facilities, transportation, equipment, or a host of other things that appear to be distinct, yet they are all connected to ensure teaching and learning is accomplished, and the team is best positioned to understand this. As Frank Betts (1992) notes, "Change has left schools playing catch-up, and it will take a whole-system approach to meet society's evolving needs" (p. 38). That statement is as true in the 21st century as it was when Betts penned it. Picking some change-agenda items while avoiding others lacks the strategic emphasis necessary to keep up with the complex change needs in education.

It is well understood that "The whole [considered as a system] is greater than the sum of its parts" (Aristotle, n.d.). This powerful statement should serve as a timeless reminder to teams that a focus on the whole system yields far greater returns than an ad hoc approach to change. As Betts (1992) notes, "the relationship among the [school districts'] elements add value to the system" (p. 40). Who is better positioned within a school district to understand this important concept than the school board–superintendent team when considering continuous school improvement? Systems thinking is not a new concept, but is often overlooked as a school board–superintendent team strength. The school board–superintendent team is well positioned for an overarching view of all elements in the system and the complex ways in which they connect throughout the district.

For the school board–superintendent team to be systems thinkers, they must recognize that day-to-day operations in the district are "not isolated [and random events,] but [rather] components of larger structures" (Senge, 1990, p. 78). There are many differing views of what it means to be a systems thinker; however, the concept of "system-wide thinking" (Senge, 1990, p. 79) is most appropriate for the school board–superintendent team. In systemwide thinking, change efforts are focused on the entire system instead of singular, more ad hoc initiatives. The systemwide perspective is steeped in the assumption that effectiveness comes from working together on a districtwide basis as opposed to working within a single school or classroom. The school board–superintendent team is well advised to lead in terms of systems thinking, taking time to understand the complex array of interconnectedness within the district. Systems thinking is imperative for both continuous school improvement and strategic planning, and meaningfully enjoins the school board–superintendent team in the important work of schools to support teaching and learning.

No doubt each school board–superintendent team can identify points of pride within the district: the types of things that make its district distinctive and represent the best of teaching and learning within its schools. However, what binds these points of pride together? In the absence of a systematic (that is, systems thinking) approach to continuous school improvement, the points of pride within the district may seem more like random acts of greatness, with little connection to each other. Further, continuous improvement that includes both internal and external review provides the essential element of quality assurance.

There are multiple bounded systems of continuous school improvement rich with validity and reliability. These systems can all have the effect of aligning members' random acts of greatness so they make systematic and organizational sense. We, as authors, recognize there is no one-size-fits-all model to continuous school improvement; however, we would like to suggest two systems that are available to boards, are bounded, and appear to be valid and reliable. We present these two models in particular because of their direct and intentional involvement of the superintendent and school board as a team—partners in improvement. These systems include the Key Work of School Boards (NSBA, 2016) and the AdvancED (n.d.a) systems approach to district performance accreditation. The NSBA (2016) framework supports the district's internal efforts, while the AdvancED model provides a third-party assessment leading to accreditation. For each model, we have provided a URL at which readers can access additional information, including access to support staff as well as a guidebook to assist in school district implementation.

Key Work of School Boards

In support of a systems-level model, the NSBA states that adopting the Key Work of School Boards supports "exploring, questioning, assessing, and working with others to improve outcomes for today's students as well as America's next generation." NSBA (2016) notes, "We have identified the core skills . . . to ensure that all students achieve at high levels." Stating the importance of systems thinking, the NSBA's (2016) Key Work framework focuses on five areas, including:

1. Vision

2. Accountability

3. Policy

4. Community leadership

5. School board–superintendent relationships

Visit National School Boards Association (www.nsba.org/services/school-board-leadership-services/key-work) for more information about this comprehensive system. (Visit **go.SolutionTree.com/leadership** to access live links to the websites mentioned in this book.)

AdvancED Performance Accreditation

Another noteworthy districtwide model for continuous improvement based on a systems approach is AdvancED Performance Accreditation (AdvancED, n.d.b). This model is the largest global resource for school improvement and includes over "34,000 schools and school systems . . . and 20 million students across the United States and 70 other nations" (AdvancED, n.d.a). The AdvancED (n.d.b) approach "aligns accreditation with accountability, emphasizing learner outcomes when evaluating institutional quality. However, it is not the outcome but the course taken over time that yields the greatest return on investment." Ultimately, the AdvancED process hopes to create a balance of systematic and systemic thinking by aligning all district systems, focusing each system on continuous improvement, and ensuring a positive integration of systems.

AdvancED provides an immense array of resources, including surveys, diagnostic tools and reviews, conferences, workshops, webinars, online learning, certification opportunities, and a research network. As a measure of its success, all U.S. Department of Defense

(DoDEA) schools worldwide participate in this five-year accreditation cycle because participating schools are "recognized across state lines . . . benefit from shared expertise and powerful professional learning . . . and personalized service" (DoDEA, n.d.).

The AdvancED (n.d.b) process is clearly a pathway to accreditation, requiring districts to:

- Meet the AdvancED standards and accreditation policies

- Demonstrate quality assurance through internal and external review (including surveys to students, staff, and parents; student performance data review; self-assessment against evaluative criteria; and evaluation of implementation by an external observation team)

- Engage in continuous improvement

The standards have direct implications for the school board–superintendent team, and throughout the continuous improvement process the team is integral to the model's success. Visit AdvancED (www.advanc-ed.org) for more information about this third-party assessment.

Either of these two bounded systems can help align the team's goals for continuous improvement. These goals should be paired with strategic planning for the future of the district.

Strategic Planning

The foundational statement concepts (values and beliefs, mission, and vision commitments) contribute much to strategic planning; however, an additional focus should be on the results that are generated from quantifiable goal statements. An easy template to consider that helps ensure quality goal setting is the use of SMART goals (Conzemius & O'Neill, 2005; Doran, 1981). Doran's (1981) original definition, as cited in Haughey (2014), includes the following characteristics.

- **Specific and Strategic:** Target a specific area for improvement.

- **Measurable:** Quantify, or at least suggest, an indicator of progress.

- **Assignable:** Specify who will do it.

- **Realistic:** State what results can realistically be achieved given available resources.

- **Time-bound:** Specify when the result can be achieved.

Use of this simple goal-setting framework ensures the management of measurable goals that are not vague. One criticism about the SMART goal technique is that is not the best fit for "long-term goals because it lacks flexibility" (Haughey, 2014).

Teams embracing the SMART technique might mitigate this with periodic updates and revision as needed.

Authors Roger Kaufman and Jerry Herman (1991) note strategic planning "in its most powerful use . . . identifies results, based upon an 'ideal' vision, to be achieved at three levels: individual, organizational, and societal" (p. 4). In this sense, foundational statements should truly be aspirational and include a focus on continuous improvement, offering stretch opportunities throughout the district that challenge the status quo and emphasize results.

The essential cornerstones of strategic planning are a focus on sound foundational statements and a bounded system of continuous school improvement (recall *bounded systems* consider and implement change to the system as a whole). The diversity of school districts across the United States and the differing teaching and learning needs within them confounds a one-size-fits-all template. Some school board–superintendent teams may be focusing resources and effort on parent involvement through collaboration, while other teams may be focusing on literacy and reading in the early grades. Both are important priorities and should be identified through a systematic process such as we have suggested. Ultimately, district priorities are endless and highly contextualized.

No matter how diverse district strategic plans are, an outcomes orientation is essential, driven by short- and long-term goals. Further, these goals should have specific, measurable objectives and clear time lines, and identify a key person or persons responsible. Three to five goals should be sufficient, with each goal having two to three objectives, to maintain a doable plan focused on clear priorities. The following example in figure 8.1 illustrates this concept.

Goal: All high schools within the district will be staffed with increasing percentages of *highly qualified* teachers.

Measurable target: In the annual report submitted July 1, the percentage of *highly qualified* teachers will increase by 5 percent.

This goal has two objectives.

1. The human resources director will facilitate developing a recruitment plan for the district that attracts highly qualified teachers. The plan will include resource implications (such as time, money, and personnel requirements). The recruitment plan must be submitted for approval to the school board–superintendent team no later than November 1.

2. Primary and secondary education directors will cofacilitate a retention plan for highly qualified teachers in the district. The retention plan must be submitted for approval to the school board–superintendent team no later than December 1.

Figure 8.1: Sample strategic plan goal.

Note that sample strategic plan statements were clear and concise. Strategic plans, guided by foundational statements and continuous improvement, need not be overly complex or they will become mired in their execution. The more complex strategic planning becomes, the less likely it is to be a *living* document, integral to a district's day-to-day operations. Keep outcomes clear, simply stated, and concise.

Professional Development Activity on Prioritization

This activity helps team members prioritize the district's needs. Prioritization practice is essential because most school board–superintendent teams will simply not have the funds or resources to address all challenges facing their school, and as a result, difficult decisions will need to be made. Teams will use a PESTLE analysis to inform their decision making and strategic planning.

Time Frame

This activity should last approximately sixty to ninety minutes.

Materials

The activity requires a facilitator, a timekeeper, PESTLE prompts (see table 8.1), pens or pencils, and paper. Teams are encouraged to edit the PESTLE prompts based on their own district characteristics and the many external factors serving as potential forces of threat and opportunity.

Table 8.1: Sample PESTLE Prompts

Political Factors	• School choice (charters, vouchers) • Negative narratives (for example, that schools aren't doing a good job of educating students and that alternatives are needed) • Changes to the skills required to be an effective teacher • Changes to curriculum, instruction, and assessment • Other: _____
Economic Factors	• Federal, state or provincial, or local government funding decisions that affect school finances • Changes in local business or industry that may affect taxing base and economic vitality

continued →

	• Socioeconomic status of parents and their ability to support the schools • Need for meal programs; backpack food programs; and before- or after-school programs, or both • Cost of providing resources: faculty, staff, or administration; basic resources; technology • Competition from neighboring school districts • Risk of highly valued teachers and administrators moving on • Other: _____
Social Factors	• Local population changes (increasing or decreasing numbers) • Demographic changes affecting schools (English language learners, special education, at risk) • Unemployment: the closure of local businesses or industry providing employment • Inability to attract educators to the community • Social networking, such as blogs, Facebook, Twitter • Parental preference—an increase in "parent power" has allowed parents more freedom of choice over their child's school • Information accessibility (accessible to staff anywhere in the world via the Internet) • Media views and district image • Other: _____
Technological Factors	• Required upgrades and changes to hardware and software • Risk of selecting the wrong technology at times of change (for example, Windows versus open source) • Public access, viruses, hackers, and so on • Management of inappropriate content • Transition from printed books to ebooks • Management of IT systems • Other: _____
Legislative Factors	• New legislation that may create risks of non-compliance, new administrative burdens, or both • Changes to child protection legislation • Early childhood (preK) schooling • Changes to teacher evaluation and school performance and educator licensure

	• Changes to funding • Other: _____
Environmental Factors	• New transportation routes as district demographics change • New dangers for pupils as the community changes • Waste and water issues • Appropriate space available for activities • Recycling and reducing material waste • Urban, suburban, and rural differences • Other: _____

*Visit **go.SolutionTree.com/leadership** to download a free reproducible version of this table.*

Process

The school board–superintendent team can conduct this exercise as one large group or include additional stakeholders such as central office and building administrators. If only the team conducts this exercise, one large-group discussion around the PESTLE prompts might suffice. If other stakeholders are included (for example, more than eight), consider the following around-the-world format.

1. After identifying one person to serve as timekeeper, the facilitator organizes the team into three table groups. Each table should have a writing utensil and paper.

2. Each table group should choose someone to serve as the table facilitator (or host) to get the conversation started and to be responsible for taking notes.

3. For ten minutes, each table analyzes two of the six PESTLE areas to reveal the factors impacting its school district and to determine how these factors affect the district and what the result of their impact might be. (For example, the first table tackles political and economic factors, the second table analyzes social and technological factors, and table three focuses on legislative and environmental factors.) Teams may like to use the prompts in table 8.1 (page 107) to guide their discussions. The table facilitator should record the group's thoughts. The timekeeper should provide a two-minute warning.

4. At the end of the ten-minute session, the table facilitator should remain in place as the rest of the group rotates to the next table. He or she will update the new group on the discussion of the previous round. Groups will then select a new table facilitator for their conversation and spend the

next ten minutes adding their thoughts to the conclusions of the previous group, using their discussion at the previous table as a guide. Again, a two-minute warning should be given.

5. Groups rotate for the third time, with the new table facilitator remaining in place. They then repeat the update and discussion steps at the final table.

6. At the end of the third session, each table will be given five minutes to prepare a very short recap of the cross-pollinated conversation about the PESTLE forces assigned to that table.

7. Groups should then reconvene, and each table will present a synopsis of its discussions for the group.

8. Once groups have discussed PESTLE forces in terms of opportunities and threats, consider their implications on current strategic planning efforts, which include both the foundational statements and continuous improvement efforts.

Results

Participation in this activity helps the team prioritize the district's needs in a strategic way that accounts for the challenging and competing needs of any complex organization. It affords the team a prioritization tool that enhances effectiveness.

Summary

Patrons in many school districts have a waning overall confidence in the school board–superintendent team's ability to provide strong academic leadership. This has been driven by many school reform efforts that include little to no roles for school board–superintendent teams other than to support the school site and building leadership. Yet, the school board–superintendent team is best positioned for systems-level thinking, understanding that everything within the district is inexorably connected. According to Peter Senge and Mary Scheetz (2016), "If we are to reconstruct our educational systems to ensure equity for all, systems thinking is an essential skill, and the habits of systems thinking must guide our actions" (p. 31).

Sound strategic planning has the potential to restore faith in the school board–superintendent team to effect positive change at the local level if two elements are focused on: strong foundational statements (such as core values or beliefs, mission, and vision commitments) and a bounded system for continuous improvement. Activities such as the PESTLE analysis can serve to jump-start and inform these imperatives.

Chapter 9

Governance and Leadership During Change

One thing is certain for the board–administrative team: it exists in a rich and complex environment of *change*. Change is constant given the many demands on an educational organization and the negative consequences associated with settling into the status quo, when so many educational organizations are "evolving and changing from one form to another" (Bäck & Lindholm, 2014, p. 77). Consequently, effective teams must not only be prepared for change, they must embrace it.

A challenge of working as part of a team is dealing with change when individual team members approach change very differently. As Senge and Scheetz (2016) note, "Systemic change is deeply personal" (p. 24). Any given change initiative may be benign for some team members (for example, "Let's just try it!") and unfathomable for other members (for example, "I'll never support this change because I know what is in store for us"). Divergent and competing individual views of change may serve to undermine the team's efficiency and effectiveness if they are not understood and anticipated. This chapter will address the forces of change at the individual and team levels to help teams better understand the concept of change and make change events predictable and manageable.

Change Implications for Individuals

There are many theories of change, and critics such as Michael Fullan (2006) note that several are simply inadequate. Ultimately, a keen understanding of change theory is only as good as its ability to positively impact the outcomes of the team's strategic plans and other important desirables. Many change theories are available to the team and might be considered as future reading to deepen knowledge and understanding (such as Ellsworth, 2000; Fullan, 2006; Senge & Scheetz, 2016; Wagner, 2001). This section does not elaborate deeply on change theory. Rather, its focus is illustrating the impact of change on the individual from an informed perspective and showing how that impact can be understood, predicted, and used to improve individual and team actions based on research, study findings, and practical experience.

When an individual experiences change, the easiest aspect of the change may be the physical change or *event* (Bridges, 2009). A *change event* is something that simply happens to people. Change events cannot usually be controlled by someone, and they may be perceived as a good change, a bad change, or something in between. However, an important emotional *transition* must also occur as an individual accepts the change and allows himself or herself to move to a future state based on the change (Bridges, 2009). The notion of a transition may take time, and is much more challenging than the change event itself.

A further, person-specific aspect is the degree of challenge the individual perceives and the time needed to come to terms with the change. For example, if part of the school board–superintendent team's strategic plan includes prioritizing the school district to be a destination of choice for students and parents, a change agenda no doubt looms ahead for the district. One goal for this strategic initiative might be to expand communication and marketing efforts regionally in hopes of attracting and recruiting new students and parents. Some members of the school board–superintendent team might accept the change as long overdue and view it as nothing more than essential next steps in an era of educational competition. However, others on the team may perceive the change priority as an ethical and moral breach, creating regional rivalry among school districts and stealing coveted resources that follow students at a time when districts should be working closely together, not competing as winners and losers. The challenge to the team is to understand that most every change, big or small, will be interpreted differently among its members. The team's goal regarding change is to successfully navigate this individual emotional journey toward its collective will. To do this, we will consider the implications of first- and second-order change, and then look at motivation's relationship with the six stages of change.

First-Order and Second-Order Change

Tim Waters and Greg Cameron (2007) introduce the terms *first-order* and *second-order change* to describe the "differing magnitudes of change" individuals experience (p. 10). Waters and Cameron assert that "the terms first-order and second-order have less to do with the actual change initiatives themselves and more to do with the *implications* of change for the individuals expected to carry out the change effort" (p. 27). First-order change is generally perceived as an extension of what is known and understood, consistent with what we value and understand and requiring little to no new knowledge or skill. For example, the team may be faced with the first-order change of wear-and-tear on facilities that will require improvements. Most teams understand the steps that will be needed to make the facility improvements. This type of change is dictated by local and state policies, guidelines, or statutes, and is a highly predictable process in most states. Second-order change, however, is perceived as letting go of all we know to be true, requiring new values and understanding as well as new knowledge and skills. Table 9.1 compares first- and second-order change perceptions.

Table 9.1: Comparison of First-Order and Second-Order Change

First-Order Change When a change is perceived as:	Second-Order Change When a change is perceived as:
Being an extension of the past	Breaking with the past
Operating within existing paradigms	Operating outside of existing paradigms
Being consistent with prevailing values and norms	Conflicting with prevailing values and norms
Requiring existing knowledge and skills to implement	Requiring new knowledge and skills to implement

Source: Adapted from Waters & Cameron, 2007.

As the school board–superintendent team considers its foundational statements, continuous improvement imperatives, and overall strategic planning, team members will need to reconcile first- and second-order perceptions of change. Using the previously stated example, a facility improvement may be predictable first-order change for most team members; however, for some it may be a second-order change. Some members may be convinced the district does not have the funds to support improvement, or they may believe the community does not support improvements at this time, especially if taxes would increase to do so. These board members may be so committed to saving resources or reducing taxes that the idea of an improvement project becomes a second-order change item. Ample evidence to support the improvement and plenty of opportunity for input into the decision can help address the concerns of those experiencing second-order change. As Bridges (1991) notes, these team members will likely exhibit "fear, denial, anger, sadness . . . [and] frustration" (as cited in Campbell, n.d.) while dealing with this change idea. Teams that recognize and accept these emotions can move best toward a healthy conclusion. In doing so, the team is able to minimize the "differential impact of leadership" (Waters & Cameron, 2007, p. 29), leading to a better understanding of the pace of change required and the most appropriate change process.

Motivation and Stages of Change

Digging deeper into the issue of why some individuals embrace change and why others resist, Fullan (2006) wisely notes, "If you take any hundred or so books on change, the message all boils down to one word: motivation" (p. 8). This is because motivation is a significant predictor of success (Ericsson, Krampe, & Tesch-Romer, 1993). One must understand motivation in the context of the individual in order to embrace change in a successful way. To best do this, let us consider typical stages of change through the lens of motivation.

James Prochaska, John Norcross, and Carlo DiClemente (1994) articulate six stages regarding the motivation to change. In thinking about change in terms of stages, do recall that change may be considered, in part, an event as well as a transition. The motivational connection comes with the emotional transition an individual makes regarding the change event. To that end, *degree* (for example, high or low) and *type* of motivation (for example, internal or external) may be different during the change process. The key outcome of understanding this concept is that the pace of change matters greatly. Pushing for rapid change may yield change results that are not sustainable with little buy-in. Slowing the pace of change too much marginalizes the relevance of the change agenda, which diminishes the willingness to stretch and grow from the change agenda.

In the following list, we adapt Prochaska, Norcross, and DiClemente's (1994) six stages of change motivation.

1. **Pre-contemplation:** At this stage, individual motivation to change is rather low. The status quo appears sufficient, so there is no desire to change. Simply stated, there is an overall lack of awareness that change is even necessary because there is no awareness that a problem even exists. This stage may be manifest in some individuals as defensiveness. Providing sufficient information to team members about the problem behind the change idea will prove helpful for those in this stage.

2. **Contemplation:** During this stage, awareness of the issues related to the change idea increases. The openness to change is greater, but commitment to change and confidence the change is worth it remain weak. Some discussion among individuals in this stage may center on the negative or unintended consequences that may arise from the change. Alternatively, a form of wishful thinking may prevail, imagining that if the status quo remains in place, somehow the problem will just go away. Allowing ample opportunity for discussion among team members about the change idea and the problems and issues supporting the change will help. Place emphasis on listening to individual viewpoints with a respect for differences and divergent views.

3. **Preparation:** As the second stage concludes and the third stage begins, a significant milestone is reached as an individual begins to favor the change idea, recognizing the benefits of the change idea outweigh holding on to the status quo. In this stage, team members make a commitment to change. Ideally, the individual is also willing to accept responsibility in his or her team role for the change as well. The individual will begin to show confidence in and commitment to the change, but overall, it still may be viewed as a weaker than stronger option. As a team member, he or she increasingly discusses the benefits of the change and make attempts to advocate for it. It is during this stage that discussion should continue among the team with regular updates about the change, to include modifications and alternatives to the change idea when needed. Regular updates will continue to strengthen the case that the change must occur. Information about the change could be data driven, based on stakeholder presentations, or the team members' experiences (for example, a tour to witness firsthand the change transformation).

4. **Action:** At this stage, individual team members let go of past values, beliefs, or norms to accept the change idea and gain new insights and knowledge as a result. They model support and acceptance for the change and often evidence enthusiasm for the change. They can successfully interact with others who may not support the change and articulate why such change is necessary and worthy of support. The greatest challenge in this stage may be the individual recognition that *real change* is hard to accomplish.

5. **Maintenance:** Individuals in this stage sustain their altered values, beliefs, and norms regarding the change idea, and little effort is needed for them to continue supporting the change. They now view the change as integrated into the organization and have personally integrated the change into their belief and value systems as well. There is a sense that the individual can reward himself or herself for embracing the change, and the change may be rewarded externally by education stakeholders as well (for example, "I'm so glad you made the tough choice to support this change!").

6. **Termination:** The change transformation is complete and a new status quo exists. Individuals are confident in the change transformation and appreciate that things are better for the district because the change was embraced. Going back to the old status quo is now unthinkable.

Individual team members will approach the six steps of change very differently given the undercurrent of motivation as a key factor. As individuals navigate the change process, it becomes anything but linear. Some may skip steps if they receive the change idea favorably. Others may move slowly through each stage before they accept the change. And ultimately, some individuals may lapse backward or remain stuck in the initial steps for a variety of reasons (like, they simply cannot let go of the status quo, or they may feel pressured by special interest groups not supporting the change). During any change event, each team member may find him- or herself in differing stages. A well-functioning team recognizes and anticipates this predictable outcome.

Organizational Change

Just as change may be considered an event as well as an individual transformation underscored by motivation, as the six stages of change motivation illustrate (Prochaska et al., 1994), the school board–superintendent team collectively experiences change through an organizational lens. The team will approach change in differing ways according to the organization's need. Some change may be well structured, such as a strategic planning process, while other change is more organic and unfolding, such as concerns from citizens demanding change. Other forms of change may be driven from the future back to the present, such as when developing the vision statement (for example, the district's dream), requiring team members to work backward to accomplish the vision. Other forms of change are present focused, working into the future (such as setting priorities, then developing goals and time lines for accomplishment). There is endless diversity of methods with which to approach change, but whatever type of change is to be addressed, the school board–superintendent team should approach it consistently from an organizational perspective. In doing so, the team builds predictability and understanding into the means by which it addresses change—a characteristic well received by the district's internal and external stakeholders.

It is noteworthy that change not only comes from within the organization, but also has external influences from the overall standing the school board–superintendent team has with the community in which it serves. Kirst and Wirt (2009) describe a three-step model regarding how a school board–superintendent team might respond to change initiatives.

1. **Null response:** The first response option is the null response, in which the team does not respond to change requests. This occurs mostly when the team's relationship with the stakeholders it serves is healthy and strong. In this case, there is often no need to embrace anything other than the status quo, and the risk is low for not responding to change-related requests.

2. **Negotiated response:** The second response Kirst and Wirt (2009) describe is the negotiated response. In this scenario, there are now "competing demands . . . over an emerging issue" (p. 141). While these do not occur

regularly for a team, they involve situations in which the team must assume the negotiator role. Change is often the outcome of a negotiated response.

3. **Prompt response:** The third and final response that Kirst and Wirt describe is the prompt response, often driven by a crisis. The crisis is "a sudden combination of threats either to the school system or its constituents" (Kirst & Wirt, 2009, p. 142). From crisis, change usually occurs because of team action. Because this is the long-understood way to affect change quickly among those with insight into organizational change, there is little wonder school board–superintendent teams are approached with persistent and ever-different crises. Armed with a greater understanding of the power of crises, the team can react to crises with predictable patterns of change in an effort to build both routines and team effectiveness.

The following professional development activity can enhance change initiatives at the individual and team levels.

Professional Development Activity on Change

This activity allows team members to investigate helping and hindering factors surrounding change events and consider how they might utilize these factors when governing. The activity builds on the force field analysis work of Kurt Lewin (1944), former director of the Research Center for Group Dynamics at the Massachusetts Institute of Technology, and Jim Dezieck (n.d.), who developed and extended important force field analysis tools for systematically addressing change.

Time Frame

The team should dedicate two or more hours to this exercise.

Materials

The team will need flip chart paper or a computer and overhead projector, sticky notes, and writing utensils.

Process

The team will do the following.

1. Identify a change initiative that will be challenging for the school board–superintendent team but is aligned with the district's strategic planning priorities.

2. Describe the change it has decided to address in one to three sentences (for example, *The district expects 100 percent of students to graduate from high school. As such, students with attendance rates of 90 percent or higher will evidence a 30 percent increase in graduation rates among all high schools during the next academic year*). Write the statement for all to see on flip chart paper or on the overhead projector.

3. Answer the following questions.

    ◆ "What are the problems requiring the change consideration?"

    ◆ "What supports are available to enable the change?"

    There may be far more problems than supports.

4. Now describe the forces that are helping or hindering the change. Examples include:

    ◆ **Helping force**—The state now monetarily rewards improved graduation rates, and the additional revenue is highly desirable to support district operations.

    ◆ **Hindering force**—A strong economy in the area has reduced the incentive to graduate, and employers are still hiring young adults without a high school diploma or a passing grade on the GED.

5. Write each helping and hindering force statement out for all to see on individual sticky notes (preferred) or on flip chart paper. Make sure each force is labeled as a help or a hindrance. This phase of the activity is not an easy task. Some team members might be reluctant to discuss hindrances, and others might believe the suggestion of hindrances is an attempt to create roadblocks to change. In each case, take time to introduce problem-based discussions so hindrances are addressed in a healthy way.

6. Sort all helping and hindering forces into two groups (for example, the helping group and the hindering group). Within each group, arrange the forces into associated clusters (for instance, some hindering forces might cluster around influences external to the schools or district, while other hindering forces may cluster around influences internal to the schools or district). The team may end up with some forces that stand alone from the clusters. Additionally, team members should have permission to offer new helping and hindering forces throughout this clustering phase, should they come to mind.

7. Review each hindering force and decide how important it is (for example, low, medium, or high). Understanding that helping forces serve to move the change initiative forward, focus on the hindering forces that can be

reduced or even removed. Then, the team should consider the importance of each force and decide how easy it would be to enact a change (such as, low, medium, or high).

8. Once the levels of importance and ease of change are determined, prioritize the changes to the hindering priorities in a way that best supports the change initiative.

9. Discuss how the helping forces support the prioritized changes to the hindering forces. To adapt this step, the facilitator should make hindering forces visually available to team members. Then, individually or in pairs, team members rate the importance and ease of change. This ensures participation among all members and encourages discussion.

10. Individuals or pairs share their ratings with the team to get an overall collective average based on feedback.

11. As a result of this activity the team now has a strong sense of the future success of the change initiative and may consider next-step actions. This will be based on an awareness of the hindering forces and the ability or willingness to move past them to implement change.

Results

Two major accomplishments come from participation in this professional development activity. First, by thinking about individual transformations (for instance, the six-step process) through helping and hindering forces associated with change, the activity provides heightened awareness about the problems behind the change initiative and supports individuals in moving past the status quo with the increased likelihood of embracing the change initiative over time. Second, next-step planning occurs for the team from an organizational level, enabling a means to address the change initiative in a systematic way through prioritizing the hindering forces in terms of importance and ease of change. Together, these accomplishments set the stage to deal with a number of change initiatives that support both the individual and the collective team.

Resistance to Change

In every organization, there will be stakeholders who simply resist change. It may be subtle and covert, or characterized by overt acts of opposition, fraught with emotion. In any case, managing resistance is a school board–superintendent team essential, as is understanding the need for educational organizations to embrace change. Resisting change can impact every aspect of the school district, not just thwarting the potential for improvement, but impacting relationships as well.

We have learned much from our work with school board–superintendent teams on how to deal with change resistance. While not all-inclusive, the following ideas may help teams caught up in the struggle of change resistance.

- Have a team consultant serve as the outside expert who facilitates the change conversation and provides a systematic means to address the change. This chapter's professional development activity (page 117) would be an appropriate model for a consultant to use.

- Invite key stakeholders to put a *face* on the change initiative, so the burden of owning the change does not rest with team members only. Consider having students, parents, or others tell how the status quo impacts them or describe why they do or do not believe the change event is important. This strategy builds a much stronger case for the problem or the attendant change because of the authentic nature of key stakeholder perspectives.

- Break the change into more manageable and incremental calls for action. Sometimes it is hard for team members to envision the entire change initiative; the status quo is simply too much to let go of. In this case, be willing to compromise on the larger change agenda for the short term by focusing on key aspects of the change now, strategically planning to more fully address the original initiative later. For example, if choice is driving an open-enrollment change initiative for the district, but it appears the team is too divided, consider interdistrict open enrollment as a first step. Although the team may not have approved a robust enrollment option allowing students from outside the district to enroll, the district has taken an important first step in piloting choice within the district for now. If a positive experience, enlarging the concept to those outside the district may be possible.

- Try to understand the nature of the resistance to the change initiative. Is it about letting go of strong beliefs, values, or assumptions? Is it that the change will require extraordinary effort (for instance, time or energy) on the person's part? Is there an outside influence such as a special interest group or undue influence causing resistance amid evidence that the change initiative should be considered? Why is there a lack of motivation to accept the change? Whatever it might be, find the root cause and work on solutions to minimize it.

Fred Lunenburg (2010) shares "the most powerful impediments to change" (p. 4).

- **Uncertainty** that is associated with giving up predictable patterns of the status quo

- **Concern over personal loss** associated with a change, such as losing authority or autonomy

- **Group resistance** against change because of established norms associated with climate and culture

- **Resistance to dependence** on others by virtue of the change. While some level of dependence is acceptable, over-dependence on others to support the change may not be well received.

- **Lack of trust** in the change environment.

- **Awareness of weakness** in the proposed change. This aspect, while a form of resistance to change, can actually benefit the team as it responds to suggestions for improvement.

As team members increasingly understand the purposes behind change and the reasons why leaders have set certain goals, they will be more likely to accept the change and assist in its fulfillment.

Summary

Change is a school board–superintendent team imperative, a constant that drives school districts. While change may be viewed as an event, the most challenging aspect of change is generally the individual transition that occurs during the change. This is confounded by the fact that any change initiative will be received differently among team members, which some view as benign and others as bold. For some, change is of the first-order nature, requiring very little from team members, while other change is more second-order oriented requiring team members to let go of their most basic values, beliefs, or assumptions. In the case of second-order change, the transition is difficult.

A systemic way to understand individual and organizational change is through a six-step process predicated on the fact that motivation underscores change. A model such as this supports predictable change and best ensures the likelihood that team members will support change. However, in some cases, change resistance will occur. Key aspects of resistance, if understood, help minimize the effects of resistance at both the individual and team levels.

Chapter 10

Dysfunctional Teams and Rogue Members

It is important to acknowledge that this entire book might have been written as a beginning effort to address the topics of this chapter: dysfunctional teams and rogue members. Dysfunctional teams and rogue members are often a combined influence or product of the same school board–superintendent team. However, it is important to state that not every dysfunctional team will necessarily have a rogue member; neither will a team with a rogue member necessarily be dysfunctional. Either one can exist without the other, and, for this reason, we treat them as separate maladies, or more specifically, distinct enemies of public school governance. In this chapter, we will define *dysfunctional* before presenting ways to heal breaches of trust, identify and deal with rogues on the team, and manage resistant team members.

Define Dysfunctional

What makes a school board–superintendent team dysfunctional? By definition, *dysfunction* means "abnormal or unhealthy interpersonal behavior or interaction within a group" ("dysfunction," 2017). The key word here is *abnormal*. To begin with, *dysfunctional* can be a confusing label, especially if it is assigned too quickly to a team that has, for a variety of reasons, not been resonating as well as it did in the recent past, disagreed on more issues of late, had some heated discussions, or not unanimously supported administrative recommendations as it did before. To be sure, each of these might be early warning signs of dysfunction, but it is not necessarily so, especially if these are recent occurrences. The same is equally true for individual team members.

Truthfully, any team may encounter some temporary operational or interpersonal mistakes anytime its actions, reactions, or both depart from its standard operating profile; however, these temporary departures are often self-correcting and frequently occur without any outside intervention, especially if the team has enjoyed a history of effective governance and leadership. However, dysfunctional actions and practices do become an issue if and when they supplant effective governance and leadership performance.

Patrick Lencioni (2002), in his book *The Five Dysfunctions of a Team*, lists dysfunctional characteristics in order of severity, with each subsequent dysfunctional characteristic being a product or result of the dysfunction that precedes it.

1. Absence of trust

2. Fear of conflict

3. Lack of commitment

4. Avoidance of accountability

5. Inattention to results

Trust, conflict, commitment, accountability, and results are essential attributes of every healthy team, including the school board–superintendent team. By stating these attributes positively, the application to effective teams becomes readily apparent because:

1. They trust one another.

2. They engage in unfiltered conflict around ideas.

3. They commit to decisions and plans of actions.

4. They hold one another accountable for delivering against those plans.

5. They focus on the achievement of collective results. (Lencioni, 2002, pp. 189–190)

Trust may well be the most important team element. Absent trust, it is challenging to accomplish any agenda, and selfish or hidden agendas may prevail. When trust prevails, however, a team can address challenging issues with divergent and differing views, and yet the team remains open to one another's opinions.

Conflict can accompany healthy dialogue, discussion, and collaboration. Admittedly, conflict can be a source of tension, but tension drives change. When team members are not comfortable with conflict, there may be a tendency to rush to a decision or outcome to avoid the discomfort associated with conflict.

Committing to decisions and plans of action is a symbolic effort to demonstrate that individual members are part of a team and are committed to moving forward together. Rarely are all team members in full and complete agreement on a decision or plan of action, but committing to move forward together is a symbolic means of demonstrating that no individual is more important than the team collectively.

Accountability among team members is a commitment to outcomes and a powerful means of modeling such expectations for all stakeholders in the district. If the team does not have accountability expectations for themselves, how can they expect the same from others within the district? Without accountability, strategic expectations are murky, and the team is often viewed as leaders piloting a rudderless ship.

Finally, a focus on achievement among team members may be the most important focus of all. When considering all the team must deal with, students must always be the first priority!

Understanding what these characteristics are representing is fairly intuitive, perhaps except for the *fear of conflict* dysfunction. Conflict is what most team members immediately consider when the topic of team dysfunction arises. Certainly, fear of conflict is a primary contributor to the dysfunctional quintet, but understanding that it really is a product of an absence of trust is imperative. Equally confusing is that engaging in unfiltered conflict is considered a positive attribute. When, if ever, is conflict within a board–administrative team good? To answer this question, the context of the term *conflict* must first be understood. A positive understanding of conflict permits a team to engage "in unfiltered and passionate debate of ideas" (p. 188), whereas a fear of conflict is exhibited by "veiled discussions and guarded comments" (Lencioni, 2002, p. 188). When conflict is translated instead to mean the unbridled sharing of differing ideas, it is suddenly clearer why it is positively or negatively a product of trust.

Understanding that the first step toward dysfunction begins with an absence of trust is crucial to unraveling and resolving the dysfunctional process. But even trust is multifaceted. It is not as simple as having confidence in someone or something. It also extends to consistent behavior and the alignment of organizational systems and structures, as well as district leadership's reputation and the school system's contribution (Covey, 2006). It is no wonder that teams steeped in dysfunction have such a difficult time digging out of the debilitating mire that accompanies it.

Recognize and Heal a Breach of Trust

Accepting that lack of trust is at the root of all dysfunction, it makes perfect sense that if there are instances where trust between team members has been compromised or trust between the superintendent and the board has been challenged, these could be at the root of the issue. However, it is also important to acknowledge that any of these may have simply been the catalyst for the breakdown of trust.

A breach of trust can occur on either side of the team. Regardless, one side or the other operates believing that the other side is in complete agreement, only to find, after a period of time, that the other side has withdrawn their support. It can also be represented by one side or the other operating in complete opposition to the established norms or values of the district.

Once a breach of trust has been recognized, the obvious first step in healing the breach is to hold a discussion between the parties and see if trust can be restored. Restoring mutual trust and respect for each other's opinions is often difficult, depending on the original catalyst for dysfunction. The initial conversation can be difficult, and it can seem more like an intervention of sorts. However, it should be initiated by the side of the team that believes it has been wronged, or by a neutral team member who recognizes that the harm has come equally from each side of the team. Sometimes these events are very personal and the emotional response is difficult to overcome. It is important that any discussions are held in a timely manner, since the longer the dysfunction continues, the more difficult it can be to get to the root of the problem.

If the team is truly in a state of dysfunction, it will be extremely difficult to correct the problem without outside intervention. Having a neutral outside facilitator assist the team in identifying the issues and exploring the remedies is preferable. Equally important to this effort is enlisting the services of someone that understands school board governance and district leadership. It is not uncommon for dysfunction to originate from a misconstrued idea of the team members' role and responsibility, and from that springboard, the issues take on a life of their own. A consultant familiar with school board governance and leadership, a school board association trainer, or even retired superintendents with a talent for team building are always great resources to exploit when confronting dysfunctional school board–superintendent team problems. A seasoned school governance expert is always a good choice to guide the reparation activities and to act as a mediator. Effective facilitators can find common ground among team members and rebuild team trust from that point.

A unique type of dysfunction can occur between a superintendent and his or her administrative team. In this situation, the relationship is less that of a collegial team and more that of CEO and subordinates. Thus, it will manifest itself differently than the dysfunction on a school board–superintendent team. One of the greatest negative indicators of superintendent–administrative team dysfunction is when an administrative team operates by *groupthink*—blindly accepting the superintendent's ideas or position because it believes another idea or opinion will not be considered if it challenges the superintendent's ideas. Groupthink is difficult to overcome without encouragement and a belief that ideas and opinions are truly valued, even if the opinions oppose the superintendent's position. The resolve to this issue begins with the superintendent encouraging others to participate without fear of reprisal (in any form), then proving that participation is valued by being willing to entertain ideas other than his or her own.

Having a system to follow as teams or facilitators begin the work of restoring balance and trust is helpful. Mark Gerzon (2006), in his book *Leading Through Conflict*, provides eight tools for mediators to use that are equally good for everyone.

1. **Integral vision:** committing ourselves to hold all sides of the conflict, in all their complexity, in our minds—and in our hearts.

2. **Systems thinking:** identifying all (or as many as possible) of the significant elements related to the conflict situation and understanding the relationships between these elements.

3. **Presence:** applying all our mental, emotional, and spiritual resources to witnessing the conflict of which we are now a part.

4. **Inquiry:** asking questions that elicit essential information about the conflict that is vital to understanding how to transform it.

5. **Conscious conversation:** becoming aware of our full range of choices about how we speak and listen.

6. **Dialogue:** communicating to catalyze the human capacity for bridging and innovation.

7. **Bridging:** building partnerships and alliances that cross the borders that divide an organization or a community.

8. **Innovation:** fostering social or entrepreneurial breakthroughs that create new options for moving through conflicts. (p. 7)

To depict these tools in the context of board–superintendent teams, the team can evidence integral vision by demonstrating a value for all perspectives and remaining open to divergent views. Individual members must also be aware of their own biases regarding the conflict and continually keep those biases in check. Systems thinking is evidenced when the team finds connections between the many elements of the conflict. As district leaders, the team is best positioned to see these intimate connections and understand the relationship among them. Presence is also important, but can be draining in terms of energy because it means being fully engaged throughout the conflict. However, conflict resolution is most sustainable when team members are fully informed by engagement.

We also believe that great teams ask great questions, particularly clarifying questions such as "Who? What? When? Where? Why?" Throughout conflict resolution, team members are advised to listen more than speak. Often, those participating in conflict are as interested in simply being heard as they are about the actual resolution. When team members do speak, they should do so with empathy and in nonjudgmental terms. Focusing on "I" statements (for example, "From what I've gathered, I believe the issue may be . . .") and minimizing "you" statements (such as "I've been told you said . . .") are effective speaking strategies regarding conflict.

Throughout the conflict process, the strategic key is to be forward thinking and not to dwell on a *rearview mirror* perspective (a focus on the past). Through this, bridging to an innovative solution occurs. Innovative solutions create new opportunities, new partnerships and alliances, and new directions stimulated by the conflict. This solution may strengthen existing partnerships or alliances, or create new ones. The goal is to identify resolutions that heal the conflict between stakeholders. Focusing on solution sustainability will be important for the team. Often, the greatest challenge to sustainable change is underestimating the pace of change. Move too quickly, and the solution may be ill-informed. Move too slow, and the solution may seem unresponsive to conflict since so much time has lapsed. Alternatively, it may be that the team is simply hoping the conflict would go away if they do not react to it. For the stakeholders of conflict to feel valued throughout this process, sustainable solutions are an imperative.

Unfortunately, restoring trust takes a lot longer than tearing it down. However, if there is a genuine desire to resolve the dysfunctional issues to allow the team to work effectively, as it is intended to, then the work to restore the trust issues is well worth the investment of time.

The conscientious team recognizes that its team members must put aside petty differences to fully address issues that prevent them from fulfilling their elected or appointed responsibilities as public officials. Dysfunction is a group problem, with each member playing either an active or passive role. This remains true, even if some are unwilling to acknowledge their dysfunctional role. Egos are difficult to tame, but if a person is ultimately reasonable, if that person's desire to work diligently on behalf of all students in public education is honest, then time spent to ensure that the team can continue the important work of decision making is worth the effort.

Identify the Rogue in the Room

Unfortunately, there may be instances when not every member on a team is reasonable. The accounts of *rogue* team members are plentiful, and the topic of the rogue is extremely popular among board members everywhere. Newspapers and social media are great places to find scenarios of bad board member behavior, as is every state school board association. Their school board field representatives are replete with examples of rogue behavior. Everyone has a story to share about the incorrigible member who will not yield to the standard of conduct and protocol that has come to represent the norm of board–administrative team decorum in a school district. It is true that the characteristics of dysfunction are applicable to the rogue member, and a rogue member may well be a major contributor to a dysfunctional board; nonetheless, a rogue member is never the sole reason for a board's dysfunction.

How is a team to identify a rogue member? First, a team member who frequently disagrees with other members of the team is not necessarily a rogue. It all depends on his or her motives and actions. As we stated earlier in this chapter, the unbridled sharing of different ideas (even disagreeing or conflicting ideas) can have a positive impact on boards (Lencioni, 2002). After all, if every team member thought identically, there would be no benefit for any board to have more than a single member. Introducing any member that does not always agree with other members will invariably be unsettling; however, it does not mean there is a rogue in the room.

Neither is the rogue member necessarily the person that asks lots of questions, or the one that consistently requires more background information for decision making than other members. These requests may be a nuisance, perceived as unnecessary, and may represent a matter that the team needs to address, either in process, or training but, in or of itself, it is not rogue behavior.

A definition is helpful to distinguish the type of person we are referring to as a rogue. *The American Heritage College Dictionary* ("rogue," 2017) defines a rogue as "an unprincipled, deceitful, and unreliable person." This definition paints a verbal image of the rogue's characteristics, and it becomes evident why we have stated that the team members in the examples above do not necessarily meet this definition.

What, then, makes a rogue a rogue, and how does a team end up with a rogue member in the first place? The following are a few attributes of rogue school board–superintendent team members.

- The individual who acts with a willful disregard for rules or board authority
- The person who uses *implied* authority to promote an idea or agenda
- The micromanager with an overinflated sense of his or her opinion and personal contributions to school governance
- The person who seeks temporary alliances to further a personal agenda
- The person who does not subscribe to a code of ethics or code of conduct

However, the qualities of rogues are not always negative. Rogue members may be very informed and opinionated on issues before the school district and may exhibit all the characteristics of *the person who can get things done*! These members may be seated on a board for a variety of reasons, including community unrest over controversial issues (such as passed or failed building projects, athletic disputes, teacher contracts, or substantial disruption to the district considered a crisis). Other factors supporting a rogue's election may include having popularity from involvement in other community organizations, or having a professional background that supports their election or appointment to a board seat. As a result, the chance of a rogue being seated on a school board–superintendent team is higher than one may first imagine.

The impact a rogue has on the entire school board, as well as the superintendent, can be catastrophic, especially if the team is ill prepared to address rogue behavior. Rogue members may cause problems for other board members, superintendents, school and district administrators, and even other school personnel, but the problem they present is ultimately a board problem, and the strategy to resolve it is solely the school board's responsibility.

Deal With the Rogue Member

How must teams deal with a rogue member? The ideal outcome for most teams containing a rogue member would be to simply remove the rogue. For superintendents exhibiting rogue behaviors, an evaluation and non-renewal pathway exists in each state to deal with the behavior if not rectified. Unfortunately, very few states have recall provisions for elected school board members. Simply stated, once the rogue acquires a seat on the school board, he or she is there for the duration of the term of office, and there is usually nothing that can be done about the rogue's elected status and his or her rights as a public official pertaining to that office unless there are serious contributing factors other than rogue behavior. However, acknowledging that nothing can be done to remove the rogue from office does not give the board permission to do nothing to control the rogue's behavior.

Teams are rarely eager to deal with rogue behavior. Some early approaches may comprise extending an olive branch to attempt to reach a level of interaction that is tolerable, or attempting to wait out the rogue behavior. These passive approaches are seldom effective, and the bad behavior will often worsen over time (McMillan, n.d.). Appealing to an "unprincipled, deceitful, and unreliable" ("rogue," 2017) person's sense of fairness is an exercise in futility. However, ignoring the issue is not an answer either. Ignoring the issue will often catapult the willful dysfunction of one member, the rogue, into a case of dysfunction for the entire team. Doing nothing damages the board's leadership reputation and can place administrators and other school personnel in an untenable position. Abandoning the school district to the whims of a rogue team member is not a tenable strategy. Ultimately, there is rarely a single action that will curtail rogue behavior. These individuals are not interested in being part of the team or considering any opinion other than their own.

Consequently, since there is no legal remedy for rogue behavior, the goal must be *containment*, not changing someone's nature. Of course, this assumes that the team has exhausted all avenues to encourage the member to operate within the acceptable governance oversight parameters. If the team determines to effect a containment strategy, it must be committed in that action and consistent with its implementation. The team's work in this regard is far more important than any individual member. It is also important that the actions in the containment strategy are not punitive. In other words, special rules cannot be levied against a rogue member that are not equally applicable for every member. Nothing can be implemented that denies the rogue the privileges and rights as a public official.

There are two possible containment strategies that school board–superintendent teams may like to use when dealing with a rogue: (1) adopting an operations compact and (2) redefining the rogue's influence. The following sections discuss both strategies.

Adopting an Operations Compact

The first strategy in containment is for the team to formally adopt a compact that defines the operating procedures and extent of board and administrative authority. Keep in mind that the compact language equally binds all team members. The language in the compact should be specific enough to address the rogue's aberrant behavior. Ideally, a school board–superintendent team develops this compact during a working session with all members present, and then formally adopts it at a public meeting where all members sign. Annually reaffirming the compact is advisable as well. In most cases, the superintendent would not have a signatory role.

There is nothing that requires the rogue to vote in favor of the compact or sign the document; however, since it will be adopted at a public meeting, there will be a record of this person's refusal. Additionally, since the action of the board is by simple majority, the fact that the rogue did not vote to approve the compact is of little consequence. If the board, by majority, approves the compact, the rogue is equally bound.

There is no reason to alarm a rogue by making a big deal out of the installation of an operations compact. Indeed, many school boards without rogues regularly approve compacts outlining how board members are expected to act in the performance of their role, finding that the extra explanation provides a good structure for both board members and superintendents. Actually, the best time to consider adopting a compact is when the board is operating well and is not reacting to a rogue's influence. Board members may consider adopting this element now, as a preventative strategy. If the rogue continues his or her bad behavior, the board has real grounds for publicly censuring the member, although from our experience, that action is seldom effective and may actually exacerbate the dysfunctional behavior. Instead of censuring, try redefining the rogue's influence.

Redefining the Rogue's Influence

The second containment strategy should be used in conjunction with adopting the board operations compact. It involves redefining the rogue's circle of influence. The three steps in this strategy are:

1. During board meetings, give the rogue's comments and suggestions only perfunctory consideration.

2. Restrict the rogue member's participation to only those acts that he or she is legally entitled to perform.

3. Strictly adhere to board operating practices outlined in the board compact. This eliminates grandstanding opportunities.

This strategy in containment is not meant to imply that the rogue should be ignored; he or she is still a board member. Additionally, rogues are not rogues all the time, so the team should not deny good ideas because of their origin. Even the most cantankerous members are given to moments of brilliance. Containment's ultimate goal is to modify the rogue's behavior, much like denying privileges to a child or assigning a time-out for misbehavior.

Earlier we stated that a rogue board member is not the superintendent's problem, and we want to reiterate that here. It is not a superintendent's responsibility to directly address a rogue board member and correct the situation. When administrator performance is adversely affected by rogue board member behavior, the superintendent's first responsibility is to take the matter to the board president for resolution by the entire board. Boards must be self-governing, and this quality is nowhere more important than when addressing rogue behavior.

However, one act that administrators may take, in conjunction with a board's behavior restriction process, is to address the line of authority for addressing questions to the administration, restricting access to buildings for board-related issues, or both. In this case, administrators should be empowered to take the appropriate steps to prevent the rogue board member from interfering in the normal school day. This is one of the most severe forms of restrictions, but in some cases this is necessary to protect administrators and school staff members from rogue behavior.

Nothing guarantees that either strategy will immediately produce the desired results, but they will enable the remainder of the board and the administration to continue governing and managing the school district despite the rogue influence. With diligence, the rogue will eventually learn that his or her voice is only that of one board member, not the voice of the board, and he or she will either comply or conform. It is not unusual for rogue behavior to disappear once a bully pulpit has been dismantled. From this point, teamwork can continue as usual.

Manage Someone Who Resists Working as a Team

Throughout this book, the emphasis has been on the importance of school board members and superintendents combining their individual experiences, skill, and intelligence into a single governance entity that we call a team. So much depends upon each member of the group contributing their share of thoughts and ideas to ensure that the team engages in not only *good* decisions and actions on behalf of school districts but the *best* decisions and actions. That is why when a member or members are reluctant to engage with the group, it is important to do everything possible to meaningfully engage them in the work of the team.

Board Members

Resistance to teamwork is frequently the result of a lack of preparation for teamwork. In school boards, a diverse group of people who generally do not have a professional education background and who are largely unfamiliar with the political environment affecting public schools, are assembled and charged with the governance oversight of public education. It is a daunting responsibility, even for individuals who do understand the complexity of the office. Preparation for the job, both as an individual board member and collectively as the assembled board, in the form of early training with their state school board association, private consultants, or by engaging in the activities in this book would encourage the formation and adherence to effective governance strategies to discourage a descent into dysfunction, individual rogue behavior, or both.

Additionally, board members may resist teamwork because they think they'll lose their personal identity to become part of another personality. The individuality that often plays a huge part of elections must give way to being only one voice among many others. Individuality disappears as soon as a board member votes; the board makes a decision and the individual vote becomes one of the pluses or minuses that determines the outcome of the motion before the board. Resolving this can be as easy as other team members making the new members feel welcome, but it can also require more efforts to intentionally engage them rather than waiting on them to feel comfortable enough to contribute.

Though their role is not as obviously team-centric on a day-to-day basis as that of the board members, superintendents must also play their part in functioning as a team. We will now discuss teamwork from a superintendent perspective.

Superintendents

Superintendents may also be unenthusiastic team players. They may feel a lack of connection to the team for a variety of reasons, and may eventually adopt a lack of conviction, not believing that being part of the team is even worth the effort. Boards must be intentional about inviting superintendents into the team. Discussing the superintendent's roles and responsibilities as a team and honoring those is an important first step. Delegating issues and concerns to the lowest appropriate level for resolution via the superintendent is also important to being a team member. Finally, inviting the superintendent's perspective on issues the board is dealing with demonstrates a value for the superintendent's views and encourages team participation

Superintendents may also find discomfort in team participation because of the vulnerability that comes from taking risks and truthfully disclosing information. Often, remaining the CEO and expert authority is safer than participating. Vulnerability related to team membership can be influenced by the superintendent's prior professional relationships with supervisors. Cases in which past relationships were healthy may serve to minimize or negate vulnerability altogether. However, when vulnerability is apparent regarding the superintendent's team membership, some simple steps can help. First, encourage ample discussion around team business and intentionally invite the superintendent's perspective. Ask follow-up questions of the superintendent that are non-judgmental (for example, ask "Help me better understand your position on this topic," rather than, "Why is that your position on this topic?"). Finally, board members might also consider regularly asking the superintendent what he or she needs to effectively discharge their duties. Often, an unmet need discourages full team participation. Finally, if the team lacks a clear focus or is dysfunctional, superintendents are much more likely to keep their educational identity separate from the board's.

In any of these situations, teams may adopt a series of steps to encourage teamwork. Teamwork begins by relying on individuals who understand team building and its benefits. Next, the team must be empowered to act, much like Lencioni's (2002) effective school board application for becoming cohesive teams. After empowerment, education and communication are the next ingredients. Transparency is important in today's school governance and leadership protocols, and communication is vital for building and maintaining trust among members. Lastly, it is equally important to accept that not everyone will join with the team. No one can mandate involvement or enforce teamwork. For some people, like rogue members, operating outside the group will forever be their norm (Kobran, 2012).

Despite much that is publicized about boards that do not operate as well as they should, or about board members that defy all the rules of ethical boardsmanship, teamwork, and effective governance, one must remember that the vast majority of school boards *get it*! These are boards whose members do their due diligence, fulfilling the role of governance oversight in the best interests of their constituencies and public education for little more than the intrinsic sense of contributing and giving back to the communities where they live and work. This important work is even further enhanced when the board and superintendent work together as a team.

Professional Development Activity on Team Commitment

This activity utilizes open-ended questions and statements to encourage vulnerability and truthful disclosure among team members. It helps the team reorient or affirm its commitment and passion for working together.

Time Frame

This activity will take the team approximately thirty to forty-five minutes to complete.

Materials

The team will need flip chart paper or an overhead screen and markers.

Process

Team members should do the following.

1. Use a flip chart or an overhead screen to brainstorm two to three of the following questions and statements—

   - I ran for the board because . . . (or) I became an administrator because . . .

   - Think of an effective team you've worked with. List what made it effective.

   - My big hope for our school board–superintendent team is to . . .

   - I learn best by . . .

   - For me to be the best teammate in decision making, I . . .

   - To be the best school board–superintendent team member I can be, I think I'm going to need . . .

   - The most effective team I've worked with had the following traits . . .

   - Two great things about my district are . . .

- The most important issues facing our school board–superintendent team are . . .

- The school board–superintendent team may not accomplish its vision, mission, or both, if . . .

2. Individually write answers to the questions and remind each other to list answers he or she would be comfortable sharing with the entire team. Encourage team members to think not just about professional team experiences, but personal opportunities too, such as experience with a church committee, or a neighborhood association.

3. Collect the responses and discuss the common themes once all team members answer the statements. Focus on each common theme shared and how it positively influences the team's work. During the discussion, team members may add to the list anything else that was not mentioned.

Usually, two to three questions or statements are sufficient for a single-setting activity. Any two that are of interest to the team will suffice. However, if this is the team's first time for such an activity, we recommend the following two questions.

- I ran for the board because . . . (or) I became an administrator because . . .

- Think of an effective team you've worked with. List what made it effective.

Results

Participation in this activity assists team members in reorienting or affirming their commitment to and passion for working together. This activity also encourages vulnerability and truthful disclosure.

Summary

The important work of public school governance relies on the collective wisdom and cooperation of superintendents and school board members who are committed to strategically meeting the challenges of public school governance and leadership together. The job is much bigger than any single individual and too important to allow dysfunctional or aberrant behavior—or both—to deter board members or superintendents from the important tasks their positions demand. Rogue team members deplete energy from the team, and periodically reaffirming the team's commitment and passion helps restore the energy teams must have to function effectively.

Chapter 11

System Evaluation Essentials

The effective school board–superintendent team spends much time and effort developing and supporting values and beliefs, vision, and mission statements (chapter 7, page 89); ensuring continuous improvement and quality assurance (chapter 8, page 101); and considering overall strategic planning (chapter 8, page 105). Ultimately, though, these important contributions are mostly input-oriented—focusing on improving team effectiveness by putting content *into* the team. In the absence of districtwide evaluation, the output side of the effectiveness equation is never addressed. Rosalie Torres, Hallie Preskill, and Mary Piontek (2005) note three important reasons for utilizing evaluation as an effective means to report and communicate organizational activities: "(1) build awareness and/or support, and provide the basis for asking questions, (2) facilitate growth and improvement, and (3) demonstrate results and be accountable" (p. 13).

Torres and colleagues' (2005) three reasons for evaluation provide a sound rationale for the school board–superintendent team placing importance on, as well as weaving together, the key concepts of foundational statements, continuous improvement, and strategic planning. This chapter more specifically addresses the essential contributions of evaluation, enabling the school board–superintendent team's ability to answer these key questions.

1. **What is working and what is not?** This question seeks to determine how varying activities within the organization connect to the intended outcomes the school board–superintendent team sets. Connection is either positive or negative.

2. **How well is this working?** This question has much to do with the fidelity of the activity to the original purpose. It is a focus on the processes implemented to accomplish an activity. This question also provides information about whether changes were made or should have been made during the evaluation period.

3. **Why does it matter?** This question assesses the rationale for the activity and addresses overall impact as well. It provides a defense for the activity and why it should be sustained, if appropriate.

Yet, these questions mean little if the team doesn't focus on *alignment*. Alignment is an intentional effort to commit district resources in support of foundational statements, continuous improvement priorities, and strategic planning outcomes. As systems thinkers of evaluation, the school board–superintendent team members can see a larger picture in which all data are connected and aligned, answering *what, how*, and *why* questions with an emphasis on resource allocation. In other words, alignment is the basis for accountability—something internal and external stakeholders alike expect of the team.

Interestingly, many teams have access to an abundance of data that would inform their evaluation efforts and provide answers to the three preceding questions. However, unless these data can be transformed into useful information, they mean little to the team. An aviation example is a particularly useful visual to demonstrate the data-to-information translation. Assume one has been invited to take a plane ride at the local airport. Before agreeing, he or she would like to assess the weather to ensure conditions are favorable. As such, that person visits the Aviation Weather Center online (www.weather.gov). Simple weather information such as in figure 11.1 illustrates how obscure data can be to the untrained eye but yet be very important.

(Extracted from FBUS31 KWNO 260801)

FD1US1

DATA BASED ON 260600Z

VALID 261200Z FOR USE 0800–1500Z. TEMPS NEG ABV 24000

FT	3000	6000	9000	12000	18000	24000	30000	34000	39000
PHX	1218	9900+24	3210+18	3109+11	3408-08	3220-17	282534	313543	304152
PRC			2706+19	2711+11	2406-09	3021-19	293435	313643	304051
TUS		2107+23	3207+17	3511+11	3117-08	3214-16	291934	313043	313552
ALS				0109+07	3215-08	3118-22	272737	273545	283654
DEN			9900+13	3520+07	3326-09	3231-23	313037	302845	293155
GJT			1105+18	2905+11	3111-09	3112-22	311738	311546	313852
PUB			900+09	3609+06	3326-08	3125-22	273337	264045	274155
BOI		1512+23	1808+17	2308+09	2323-10	2121-23	221838	232245	263751
LWS	9900	2007+23	2107+16	2209+08	2122-10	2327-23	242539	242448	254252

Figure 11.1: Sample wind and temperature data for higher altitudes.

Source: National Oceanic and Atmospheric Administration (NOAA), 2017.

While figure 11.1 is rich with wind-speed data, it may not mean much to the untrained eye in terms of useful information. Essentially, it is not useful to a reader. However, if we translate these important data into useful information, we know that the local airport will have temperatures of 43 degrees Fahrenheit, with 40 percent humidity, northeast winds at five miles per hour, and ten miles of visibility. Perfect weather for flying! The key to the usefulness of these data lies in their translation to meaningful information. When school districts collect data for the purpose of evaluation, they often fall prey to similar challenges with the data they collect—gathering excellent and copious data, but failing to make meaningful information from them.

Data are often collected within the organization and shared as aggregated tallies, means, standard deviations, percentages of increases and decreases, and inferential data such as growth scores. Sometimes, a grand leap is made from these types of data to an informational outcome, such as when a school district earns a grade level "B." But what does a "B" mean, how did the district earn it, and why does it even matter? All these are questions that a focus on evaluation can assist with by easing the data-to-information transition and supporting informed team decision making. In this chapter, we will discuss how to develop a data system and transform data into useful information. We will also delve into how to communicate effectively during evaluation, and how to use evaluation information.

Developing a Data System

Given that every district is unique, data sources and collection systems will vary to appropriately reflect the distinctiveness of the district (such as locale, size, poverty level, and academic focus). Yet, some common performance indicators may prove useful as the school board–superintendent team determines its data priorities across the district. Remember, data priorities should be tied to the team's budget priorities, foundational statements, continuous improvement efforts, and strategic planning. A data system could be in the form of existing data, such as student performance data found in Excel spreadsheets or within the state's database, or new data, such as a climate survey to assess overall morale. Simply pick a system that is most likely to provide the school board–superintendent team with *meaningful* information.

The following bulleted lists contain representative data indicators that teams may use to stimulate conversations about distinct data priorities. It is helpful when the same source can be utilized each year, so that year-to-year (for instance, calendar or fiscal) comparisons can be made. Student performance data indicators include:

▪ Attendance rates

▪ Graduation and dropout rates

- Promotion and pass rates
- Test or achievement scores (for example, local, state or provincial, national)
- End-of-course assessments
- Growth data (such as proficient, basic, or below basic)
- College and career readiness
- Twenty-first century learning skills readiness

School-level data indicators include:

- Enrollment characteristics (such as by class, grade, or school)
- School demographics (like disaggregated groups such as race or ethnicity, socioeconomic level, school locale, and size)
- Rigor of curriculum
- Discipline referrals including exclusions (such as suspension and expulsion)
- Climate and culture survey, focus group feedback, or both (for instance, appraising teaching or learning expectations, levels of collaboration, morale, quality of work expectations, and shared vision)
- School improvement efforts
- Professional development for faculty, staff, administration, or all of them
- Leadership and teaching evaluations
- Parent involvement

District-level indicators include:

- Goal statements informed by foundational statements, continuous improvement, and strategic planning
- State and federal accountability measures (for instance, adequate yearly progress)
- Currency of policy and guidelines to support operational flexibility, high-quality teacher recruitment and retention, and ineffective teacher intervention
- Resources allocated to support improved teaching and learning as well as those students not making progress
- Technology support as a teaching and learning tool

- Board and superintendent evaluation
- Frequency of school board–superintendent team professional development
- Community involvement to include business or industry partnerships

The actual configuration of these data indicators and options for the system of collection are limitless. What is important is that "Data need to be presented in a clear, concise manner to enhance readability and understanding" (National Center for Chronic Disease Prevention and Health Promotion, 2013, p. 6).

Transforming Data to Information

A great starting place to think of transforming district data to information begins with a bounded inquiry system, such as the Annenberg Institute for School Reform's inquiry cycle (Barnes, 2004). (Recall from chapter 8, *bounded systems* thinking considers the system as a whole.) This six-step cycle as adapted for school board–superintendent teams in figure 11.2 provides teams with a context for collecting data and a focus on actions to be taken as a result of those data.

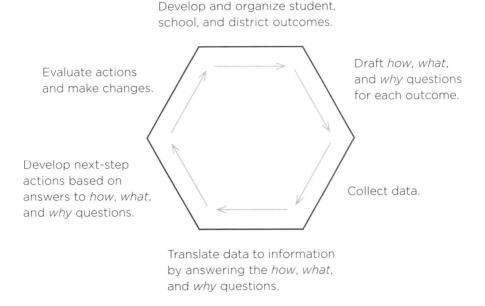

Source: Adapted from Barnes, 2004.

Figure 11.2: The inquiry cycle.

The first step in utilizing the inquiry cycle is to develop and organize desired outcomes. Generally, teams will not be starting from square one. Rather, they may just need to compile existing outcomes and identify any gaps, or simply affirm what has already been established. Prioritizing outcomes is also encouraged during this step. Next, *how, what,* and *why* questions can be developed to ensure teams collect quantifiable and informing data. This phase is extremely important because sound leadership is underscored by sound questions. The professional development exercise in this chapter will help develop your questioning talents. After teams agree on the appropriate questions, they will collect data. Often, existing data are available, but new data may be required as well. Aligning the data with the appropriate questions serves to turn data into useful information. Often, teams will state, "We're drowning in data!" but not know how to interpret or utilize it. This useful step negates this long-standing concern. Teams then develop and prioritize action steps based on the data-to-information transition. Finally, evaluation and changes occur periodically as needed, leading to the first step of the cycle once again: the outcomes now desired as a result of the recent evaluation.

The cyclical model is helpful to those teams already engaged in evaluation as well as to those just beginning. For those just beginning, it provides a bounded system to guide informed decision making. For teams already engaged in regular evaluation, elements such as asking *how, what,* and *why* questions may provide differing or deeper insight into existing data-to-information transitions.

The cyclical nature of the inquiry cycle means teams can repeat steps again and again as the situation requires. Some steps may need to be repeated and some steps focused on more than others, depending on the situation. Evaluation changes, new priorities, and even how workload effort is distributed may all impact a school board–superintendent team's data collection and evaluation efforts. Ultimately, the inquiry cycle supports the team in its efforts for improvement on selected priorities while sustaining positive outcomes identified from the evaluation process.

Professional Development Activity on Evaluation

Central to sound evaluation, and more specifically, meaningful accomplishment of the inquiry cycle, is the ability to ask good *what, how,* and *why* questions. This activity helps the team review its *what, how,* and *why* questions to gain maximum information from collected data.

Time Frame

The team should plan one hour to complete this activity.

Materials

The team will need a facilitator, its district's foundational statements, pens or pencils, and paper.

Process

After identifying a desirable outcome from the foundational statements, continuous improvement planning, or strategic plan that the team would like to evaluate, teams should do the following.

1. Review the following three question types and the team's intended purpose for each activity.

   ◆ **What is working and what is not?** This question clarifies how an activity connects positively or negatively to the intended outcomes the school board–superintendent team set.

   ◆ **How well is this working?** This question focuses on the process or processes implemented to accomplish an activity, including whether changes were made or should have been made.

   ◆ **Why does it matter?** This question assesses the rationale for the activity and addresses overall impact as well.

2. Write *what*, *how*, and *why* questions (approximately three per question category) for the outcome the team intends to evaluate. It is important to note that not every question must begin in *what*, *how*, or *why* (see the following example). The facilitator can assign a category of questioning (for example, what, how, or why) to teams of two or three, then share and edit with the larger group, or the team can do this as a school board–superintendent team. For example, let us assume the team wants to evaluate whether district attendance has improved over the past academic year, based on its strategic plan. The following questions might be appropriate.

   ◆ **What?** What schools, on average, have evidenced improved attendance rates? What grades per school, on average, have evidenced improved attendance rates? Is there a difference in attendance rates per school among gender, socioeconomic status, or qualifying categories (for example, special needs, gifted or talented, or English learner)?

   ◆ **How?** Did the new attendance incentive program (for instance, to opt out of final exams for good attendance) for high school students increase attendance? How did parents perceive the new attendance expectations at each developmental level (for example, elementary, middle, and high school)? How did the home-visit initiative for students missing more than eight days impact attendance after the home visit? Did the mid-year change to make a home visit after eight days instead of ten days impact student attendance?

- ◆ **Why?** Was the additional time required for home-visitations worth the investment? Because of the heightened attendance expectations, did more students or parents opt to homeschool? Was the missed experience of preparing for and taking a final exam worth the incentive of opting out?

3. The National Center for Chronic Disease Prevention and Health Promotion (2013) has a checklist for assessing evaluation questions, adapted into the following list of ten criteria. The team (or smaller groups reporting back to the team for consensus) should ask if the individual evaluation questions, written earlier, meet the following criteria. If not, the question or questions should be edited to meet the criteria, or the team should justify its inclusion.

   a. Stakeholders who can act on the evaluation finding and those affected by such findings will be engaged in answering the question.

   b. Stakeholders will be engaged in next-step actions based on the answer to the question.

   c. The question supports the team's overall change agenda.

   d. The question is directly linked to goals and objectives, if applicable.

   e. The question reflects the district's vision, mission, and core values.

   f. Answering the question will transform data to provide useful information to stakeholders.

   g. The answer can be obtained ethically and respectfully (for example, no harm done to an individual such as breach of confidentiality).

   h. Sufficient resources (for example, time, money, personnel) are available and able to be directed toward answering the question.

   i. The question may be answered in an acceptable and usable time frame.

   j. This question, in addition to other questions, provides a complete picture of the activity selected to evaluate.

4. Armed with questions meeting the ten criteria, or justifications for those not meeting the criteria, the facilitator is now ready to delegate the questions to appropriate stakeholders for data collection as part of the inquiry cycle. A process such as this is recommended as a means to evaluate all interested activities.

Results

Participation in this activity helps team members strengthen their ability to ask good *what*, *how*, and *why* questions. Asking good questions is tantamount to effective inquiry about what is working and what is not within a school district.

Communicating Strategically During Evaluation

Effective evaluation also includes a strategic emphasis on communicating results. An effort to share the results of the school board–superintendent team's evaluation process reaches a host of internal and external stakeholders to the district and informs them of the district's progress. Included in the internal stakeholder group might be faculty, staff, students, and administrators. External stakeholders might include parents, community members (many of which may have no school-aged children and may not realize the benefit of their tax dollars supporting the district), business and industry leaders, and elected officials. However, "Engaging [stakeholders] begins with listening. It's not uncommon for an educator's view of success to differ significantly from the views of a taxpayer, parent, or business leader" (AASA, 2002, p. 28). As such, always make time for stakeholder feedback when presenting evaluation results.

Teams should plan to share their results in verbal and written forms, as well as combinations of the two. A verbal presentation of results, for example, might be accompanied by a PowerPoint presentation. Charts, graphs, and other visual aids are generally preferred over data tables because they are easier to draw meaning from and are more user-friendly overall. Written communication of the evaluation outcomes should be prepared for the district's website and made easily accessible to site visitors (no more than one click away from the home page).

Both written and verbal communication should be logically organized and free from errors. Whenever possible, teams should consider the audience it will be presenting its evaluation findings to and tailor the message to this audience, since information needs may vary. For example, presenting findings internally to faculty, staff, or administrators will have a different delivery and focus than a presentation to a community group. One compelling difference is that faculty, staff, and administrators likely contribute to many of the evaluation activities and have a direct and vested interest in the outcomes. As such, a detailed presentation that includes the full report, an executive summary, and associated data or information would be appropriate. Community members, on the other hand, might benefit from a focus that demonstrates the district is accountable to itself and others for its educational priorities with a more general and less data-centric focus. In this case, an executive summary or a focus on success stories with next-step plans to address challenges would be appropriate. In either case, present the positive outcomes as well as the negative, challenging, or even unexpected outcomes of the evaluation process, all of which inform next-step planning.

Whether a verbal or written format for the report is to be used, deciding what to include is an important first step in communicating results. There is no one-size-fits-all outline. The following components might prove helpful.

- Consider a twelve-point font type so the report is readable.

- Apply bolded headings consistently to organize the report.

- Do not crowd the pages of the report; use white space to ensure report readability.

- Provide an introduction explaining the report's format and its general content.

- Develop summary statements for each of the six steps in the inquiry cycle.

  - Include all *how*, *what*, and *why* questions and order them the same in any section of the report that addresses the questions.

  - In the data collection summary statement, note the methods used to collect data (for instance, parent or student surveys, or existing data collected by the state).

  - In the data-to-information summary statement, note general procedures used to answer the questions (such as means, simple tally, or growth score comparisons).

  - Present data and other supplemental information requiring much space in appendices to keep the evaluation report as concise and focused as possible.

- Consider mentioning suggestions for future evaluation based on the current evaluation cycle as part of a concluding statement.

- Once the preceding steps have been accomplished, develop an executive summary, which typically summarizes the key findings in an easily understood format. The executive summary can usually stand alone as a brief version of the evaluation report, and may also be included in the front of the larger report, positioned before the formal introduction.

To ensure accuracy, circulate drafts of the report to key stakeholders in the evaluation process—those who contributed to varying steps in the inquiry cycle. This is especially helpful as the school board–superintendent team interprets the process's positive, negative, and unintended outcomes. The perspectives of the key stakeholders can inform team findings and conclusions.

Timing may also need to be a consideration. Decide whether certain stakeholders should receive the report prior to its public release. The key advantage to sharing the report prior to official release is allowing select individuals time to digest findings and prepare a thoughtful response to the findings.

Using Information From Evaluation

While the preceding section addresses communicating evaluation outcomes to a variety of stakeholders, it is equally important that the evaluation outcomes inform next steps. This can only be accomplished by *using* the information. The school board–superintendent team must encourage using evaluation findings and conclusions. The National Center for Chronic Disease Prevention and Health Promotion (2013) offers several actions, which we adapted, to ensure usage.

- Conduct regularly scheduled meetings or forums with evaluation stakeholders internal and external to the district. This real-time sharing adds deeper meaning to the findings and conclusions, because it is not a retrospective focus, but rather intentionally forward thinking about next-step improvements, informed by evaluation reporting.

- Take advantage of regularly scheduled meetings to address specific findings and recommendations in the evaluation report, as opposed to covering the entire report in a single setting.

- Focus stakeholders on how they might apply the evaluation findings in their own professional settings.

- Coordinate, document, and monitor improvement efforts related to the evaluation report over time.

- Develop multiple reporting formats best suited for specific stakeholder needs.

As teams become well versed in using and communicating the information resulting from data, their data-collection efforts will become more meaningful, relationships with stakeholders will be improved, and trust in the local team's ability to assess situations and effect results will increase.

Summary

It is a moral and ethical imperative for the school board–superintendent team to focus evaluation efforts on foundational statements, continuous improvement, and strategic planning. Three key questions form the cornerstones of sound evaluation.

1. What is working and what is not?
2. How well is this working?
3. Why does it matter?

These key questions have the effect of transforming data into useful information; however, question development is only a portion of what a systematic approach to evaluation includes.

The inquiry cycle provides a strong basis for evaluation planning. This six-step model includes (1) identifying and organizing student, school, and district outcomes; (2) developing *how*, *what*, and *why* questions; (3) collecting data; (4) translating data to information; (5) developing next-step actions; and (6) evaluating actions, including making necessary changes. A helpful professional development activity in this chapter provided a rubric to evaluate *how*, *what*, and *why* questions.

Additionally, evaluation efforts must include strategic communications to a host of internal and external district stakeholders. Whether verbal or written presentations of the evaluation are being considered, a report format should be considered that is well organized, user-friendly, and objective (for example, includes positive, negative, and unintended outcomes).

Finally, the school board–superintendent team must ensure the information gleaned from the evaluation report is actually being used. A variety of means such as utilizing time during regularly scheduled meetings as well as periodic forums, depending on the stakeholder group, can accomplish this. The key is to focus stakeholders on how they might apply the evaluation finding in their own professional setting.

Chapter 12

The Future of the School Board–Superintendent Team

The challenges of 21st century education are overwhelming, and critics grapple over the methods for providing quality educational opportunities within an optimal educational environment. At the heart of all these discussions are the men and women who wrestle with these issues at the local level as superintendents and school board members. They face these challenges willingly, forever advancing the cause of education within their districts. As Daniel R. Davies and Fred W. Hosler (1949) state:

> The challenge of board membership lies in the realm of educational statesmanship, in keeping free of petty detail work in order to sense trends, needs, and aspirations. The challenge to the board is to chart the course of American education, to approve the policies which will aid educators in keeping to the course, and to check up from time to time on how matters are progressing. Accordingly, the mechanics and details of administration are delegated to the superintendent of schools. (p. 14)

Davies and Hosler's (1949) quote represents some very general role and responsibility descriptions that superintendents and school board members commonly share across the United States. In simple terms, this convivial, complementary relationship that Davies and Hosler (1949) suggest establishes an operational framework that, in turn, allows the board–superintendent team to provide governance and leadership within and through its respective obligations to public education. In their book *The Challenge of School Board Membership*, Davies and Hosler (1949) further explain this relationship, and, though written decades ago, the information is just as relevant today as it was when the book was published. The basic relationship between superintendents and school board members remains philosophically the same. This chapter will discuss how to continually strive for the ideal "universal" relationship between the school board and superintendent, remind readers of the purpose of the school board–superintendent team, and hypothesize about the future influences on the team.

In Search of the Universal Relationship

Most school board–superintendent teams, and the communities they serve, assume that the school board members and superintendents rise to their appointments with the goal of working together in harmony to meaningfully serve their communities. Unfortunately, an all-inclusive instruction manual for superintendents and school board members that authoritatively describes *everything* they need to know to fulfill their responsibilities successfully has yet to be written. School governance research is not plentiful, and as political scientist and author William Howell (2005) observes, "more is known about the operation of medieval merchant guilds than about the institutions that govern contemporary school districts" (p. 15). Additionally, as the preceding chapters note, although the essential leadership and governance processes that superintendents and school board members observe are the same, actual practices can vary substantially from one school district to another. These operational differences—many driven by local traditions and past practices, as well as by the district's distinct culture and climate—often interfere with the school board–superintendent team's attempts to modify relationships and processes and can actually damage the overall relationship.

It is beneficial to periodically, but intentionally, assess the relationship to ensure that the team is still functioning as well as it seems to be. It is not uncommon for a school board–superintendent team to realize small performance glitches that creep into the team's overall character, and it can happen to the best of teams with the strongest of professional relationships. Taking for granted that a well-functioning team will always be so is an error. Remaining viable and effective in governance and leadership requires constant maintenance to ensure that the team remains solidly grounded and performance-ready. As writer and consultant Doug Eadie (2005) states:

> Human relationships are always fragile, and this one is no exception; indeed, the forces working against a healthy board–superintendent partnership are daunting. For one thing, today's volatile environment—socially, economically, politically—bombards your board and superintendent with a never-ending stream of complex issues. . . . Grappling with them can, over time, cause enough stress and strain to seriously fray this most precious partnership. (pp. 71-72)

A Team With a Grand Purpose

Shouldering the responsibility for providing public education opportunities to benefit approximately 49.5 million students through the employment of 3.1 million teachers in over one hundred thousand primary and secondary schools throughout the United States (National Center for Education Statistics, n.d.), superintendents and school board members methodically perform what many have described as a thankless job. Add to those numbers millions of support personnel, such as bus drivers, food service, daily maintenance, classroom aides, security personnel, health professionals, and others, and it is quickly and inarguably understood that public education is collectively the largest employer in the United States. Additionally, when one considers the numbers of school board members across the nation, public education governance oversight is easily represented and accomplished by the largest number of public officials in the United States (CareerOneStop, 2014). It is little wonder education persists as a top priority for the United States among so many stakeholders, groups, agencies, and organizations.

People enter public education as a career and as a public service for a variety of reasons, but to be successful, personal interests must meld with the purposes for education that have been outlined in the various state constitutions and refined within respective communities and school districts. There has never been a greater need or a greater calling for individuals to accept the responsibility to carry that mantle forward. It does require leadership in governance and management and, therefore, it will require leaders.

Joel A. Barker (n.d.), a well-known futurist, defines a leader as "a person you will follow to a place you wouldn't go by yourself." That really is what leadership represents, regardless of whether the leader is a superintendent wrestling with day-to-day issues in the school district, or a school board member who brushes against public education at regular intervals. The magic we recognize as leadership is recognizing where the school district would be if superintendents and board members were not willing to lead them.

Future Influences and Challenges

Former *New York Times* education reporter Gene I. Maeroff (2011) notes the "vision of the school board is synonymous with democracy in the minds of people" (p. 30). We agree and further maintain that the school board's important role in concert with the superintendent will continue. As the most basic governmental unit, the school board–superintendent team is best positioned to receive and consider the educational concerns of a community as well as to make meaning of state and national legislation and policy. Del Stover (2010) also agrees when he states, "Local control of the public schools remains an enshrined tradition of American democracy, and the vast majority of the public—as well as state and federal policymakers—want it to stay that way" (p. 26).

In addition to local boards persisting in the future, we believe the following considerations will also influence and shape the team.

- Confidence in local control as the lever of effective change will continue to wane until the school board–superintendent team inserts itself into reform conversations and takes distinctive actions for sustainable and continuous improvement. The team's role as the system-level leaders, with keen understanding that everything is connected, positions them well for meaningful next steps in the reform conversation.

- Education critics own the education reform narrative from a political point of view, and persistently frame the narrative in terms of a crisis in order to quicken the pace of change (Hill, 2015; Ozimek, 2015; Schneider, 2016). Boards and superintendents must consider governance and leadership strategies that are data driven, student focused, improvement laden, and strategic to minimize the crisis narrative and restore trust for improvement at the local level. Controlling the pace of change will also be imperative for sustainable solutions to emerge, not quick-fix solutions.

- Low voter turnout from apathy and off-election cycles will continue to influence election to the board. Greater consideration should be given to including board elections in general election cycles, even at the risk of tying such elections to partisan politics. Doing so may increase the chances that diverse and representative board members are elected.

- Professional development for most U.S. states is not a requirement of holding office, yet every shred of evidence suggests professional development is key to governance and leadership effectiveness (Blumsack & McCabe, n.d.; Michigan Association of School Boards, n.d.; Roberts & Sampson, 2011). Professional development, in which all team members participate, should be considered a requirement for board members and superintendents alike.

- Choice is here to stay. Families demand choice and alternatives, and education is no exception. The school board–superintendent team needs to work comfortably and proactively in an era of choice to meets the demands of a citizenry wanting an increased voice and stake in day-to-day operations within the district.

- School boards and superintendents must include constituent training programs in their governance arsenal and enlist grassroots initiatives that will further educate and inform lawmakers who can confidently support public education and the professions that are its foundation.

As board members and superintendents work to embrace the change-fraught nature of contemporary education, insert themselves as needed into local reform conversations, and develop the skills they need to equip themselves with leadership and governance abilities, the future of the school board–superintendent team as a unit for effecting meaningful change is bright.

Professional Development Activity on the Future of the Team

This final professional development activity helps teams visualize their future by use of simple imagery. It allows team members to reflect on the current status of the team and share their hopes and goals for how they would like the team to function in the future.

Time Frame

This activity will take fifteen to forty-five minutes to complete, depending on the number of questions asked by the facilitator.

Materials

For this activity, all team members must view figure 12.1 (page 154). Teams will also need a facilitator.

Process

After reviewing the visual of the leadership tree (figure 12.1, page 154), the team does the following.

1. A facilitator asks the following questions (teams might choose to answer only one or two depending on time and interest).

    *   Thinking of the school board and superintendent as a team, what role do I contribute as a team member as illustrated by a child on the leadership tree? Why?

    *   Thinking collectively about the school board–superintendent team, which child best represents our team currently? Why?

    *   Thinking of our school board–superintendent team collectively, which child best describes where we should be in the future? Why?

2. The facilitator then asks each team member to volunteer his or her answer or answers and rationale. Other team members may ask questions for clarity, but should not judge any answer.

Source: © 2014 Bradley V. Balch.

Figure 12.1: The leadership tree.

*Visit **go.SolutionTree.com/leadership** to download a free reproducible version of this figure.*

3. The facilitator concludes by restating the common areas of strength, challenge, or both that team members shared and how this information might help the team now as well as in the future.

Summary

The supreme challenge to the school board–superintendent team is not really anything that deals with the position or business of either side, but rather the *mechanics* of governance and leadership within roles and responsibilities. It is about doing a job together that is greater than anyone can accomplish without the others. We believe local school boards and superintendents have much hope for a bright future if they are willing to work as a team. Optimistically, we posit the basics of this book lay a groundwork for effective and productive team relationships that build on the great traditions and shortfalls of U.S. education, envisioning a hopeful, yet ever-changing future.

[references and resources]

AdvancED. (n.d.a). *About us*. Accessed at www.advanc-ed.org/about-us on June 3, 2017.

AdvancED. (n.d.b). *Accreditation*. Accessed at www.advanc-ed.org/services/accreditation on October 9, 2016.

Alexander, K., & Alexander, M. D. (2012). *American public school law* (8th edition). Belmont, CA: Wadsworth.

American Association of School Administrators. (n.d.). *Code of ethics: AASA's statement of ethics for educational leaders*. Accessed at www.aasa.org/content.aspx?id=1390 on January 30, 2017.

American Association of School Administrators. (2002). *Using data to improve schools: What's working*. Arlington, VA: Author.

Aristotle. (n.d.). *Aristotle, metaphysica quotes*. Accessed at www.quotes.net/quote/38481 on September 26, 2016.

Bäck, E. A., & Lindholm, T. (2014). Defending or challenging the status quo: Position effects on biased intergroup perceptions. *Journal of Social and Political Psychology*, *2*(1), 77–97.

Barker, J. A. (n.d.). *Joel A. Barker quotes*. Accessed at www.brainyquote.com/quotes/authors/j/joel_a _barker.html on November 7, 2016.

Barnes, F. D. (2004, April). *Inquiry and action: Making school improvement part of daily practice*. Providence, RI: Annenberg Institute for School Reform at Brown University. Accessed at www .annenberginstitute.org/sites/default/files/product/276/files/SIGuide_intro.pdf on January 30, 2017.

Betts, F. (1992). How systems thinking applies to education. *Educational Leadership*, *50*(3), 38–41.

Blumsack, K., & McCabe, T. (n.d.). 7 signs of effective school board members. *American School Board Journal*. Accessed at http://www.asbj.com/TopicsArchive/SchoolGovernance/7-Signs-of-Effective -School-Board-Members.html on June 3, 2017.

Board of Regents of State Colleges v. Roth, 408 U.S. 564 (1972).

Bridges, W. (1991). *Managing transitions: Making the most of change*. Reading, MA: Addison-Wesley.

Bridges, W. (2009). *Managing transitions: Making the most of change* (3rd ed., rev. and updated). Philadelphia: Da Capo Press.

Brower, R. E., & Balch, B. V. (2005). *Transformational leadership and decision making in schools*. Thousand Oaks, CA: Corwin Press.

Campbell, H. (n.d.). *How to reduce resistance to change.* Accessed at http://blog.commsmasters.com /how-to-reduce-resistance-to-change on June 3, 2017.

CareerOneStop. (2014). *Occupations with the largest employment.* Accessed at www.careerinfonet.org /oview3.asp?printer=&next=oview3&level=overall&optstatus=101000000&id=1&nodeid=5& soccode=&stfips=00&jobfam=&group=1&showall=no on November 7, 2016.

Carter, G. R., & Cunningham, W. G. (1997). *The American school superintendent: Leading in an age of pressure.* San Francisco: Jossey-Bass.

Coleman, J. (2013, May 6). Six components of a great corporate culture. *Harvard Business Review.* Accessed at https://hbr.org/2013/05/six-components-of-culture on January 30, 2017.

Community Schools of Frankfort. (n.d.). *Mission and vision.* Accessed at www.frankfortschools.org /content/mission-vision on January 30, 2017.

Conger, J. A., & Kanungo, R. N. (1998). *Charismatic leadership in organizations.* Thousand Oaks, CA: SAGE.

Conzemius, A., & O'Neill, J. (2005). *The power of SMART goals: Using goals to improve student learning.* Bloomington, IN: Solution Tree Press.

Covey, S. M. R. (2006). *The speed of trust: The one thing that changes everything.* New York: Free Press.

Daft, R. L. (2005). *The leadership experience* (3rd ed.). Mason, OH: Thomson/South-Western.

Davies, D. R., & Hosler, F. W. (1949). *The challenge of school board membership.* New York: Chartwell House.

Department of Defense Education Activity [DoDEA]. (n.d.). *Accreditation.* Accessed at www.dodea .edu/Accreditation/why.cfm on June 3, 2017.

Derbeko, P. (2014, September 27). *In the land of dead documents.* Accessed at www.linkedin.com /pulse/20140927214901–2065649-in-the-land-of-dead-documents on January 30, 2017.

Dervarics, C., & O'Brien, E. (2011, January). *Eight characteristics of effective school boards: Full report.* Alexandria, VA: Center for Public Education. Accessed at www.centerforpubliceducation .org/Main-Menu/Public-education/Eight-characteristics-of-effective-school-boards/Eight -characteristics-of-effective-school-boards.html on January 30, 2017.

Dezieck, J. (n.d.). *Planning for change: The force field tool.* Accessed at http://hrweb.mit.edu/learning -development/learning-topics/change/articles/force-field on January 30, 2017.

Doran, G. T. (1981). There's a S.M.A.R.T. way to write management's goals and objectives. *Management Review, 70*(11), pp. 35–36.

DuFour, R., DuFour, R., Eaker, R., Many, T. W., & Mattos, M. (2016). *Learning by doing: A handbook for Professional Learning Communities at Work* (3rd ed.). Bloomington, IN: Solution Tree Press.

dysfunction. (2017). In *Merriam-Webster's online dictionary.* Accessed at www.merriam-webster.com /dictionary/dysfunction on January 30, 2017.

Eadie, D. (2005). *Five habits of high-impact school boards.* Lanham, MD: Scarecrow Education.

Ellsworth, J. B. (2000). *Surviving change: A survey of educational change models.* Syracuse, NY: Clearinghouse on Information & Technology.

Ericsson, K. A., Krampe, R. T., & Tesch-Romer, C. (1993). The role of deliberate practice in the acquisition of expert performance. *Psychological Review, 100*(3), 363–406.

Fullan, M. (2006, November). *Change theory: A force for school improvement* (Seminar Series Paper No. 157). Jolimont, Victoria, Australia: Centre for Strategic Education. Accessed at http://michaelfullan.ca/wp-content/uploads/2016/06/13396072630.pdf on January 30, 2017.

Gemberling, K. W., Smith, C. W., & Villani, J. S. (2000). *The key work of school boards guidebook.* Alexandria, VA: National School Boards Association.

Gerzon, M. (2006). *Leading through conflict: How successful leaders transform the differences into opportunities.* Boston: Harvard Business Review Press.

Glass, T. E., Björk, L., & Brunner, C. C. (2000). *The study of the American school superintendency, 2000: A look at the superintendent of education in the new millennium.* Arlington, VA: American Association of School Administrators.

Haughey, D. (13 Dec 2014). *A brief history of SMART goals.* Accessed at https://www.projectsmart.co.uk/brief-history-of-smart-goals.php on June 3, 2017.

Heathfield, S. M. (2015, August 23). *Play well with others: Develop effective work relationships.* Accessed at www.thebalance.com/developing-effective-work-relationships-1919386 on January 30, 2017.

Hill, S. (2015). This is not a test: A new narrative on race, class and education. *Perspectives on Urban Education, 12*(1). Accessed at http://www.urbanedjournal.org/archive/volume-12-issue-1-spring-2015/not-test-new-narrative-race-class-and-education-jos%C3%A9-vilson-ch on June 3, 2017.

Howell, W. G. (Ed.). (2005). *Besieged: School boards and the future of education politics.* Washington, DC: Brookings Institution Press.

Indiana School Boards Association. (2010). *Code of ethics.* Accessed at http://isba-ind.org/wp-content/uploads/2015/07/CODEthic1.pdf on March 24, 2017.

Indiana School Boards Association. (2015). 2015 school board/superintendent profile summary. *The Journal, 61*(5).

Institute of Education Sciences, National Center for Education Statistics. (n.d.). *Common Core of data.* Accessed at https://nces.ed.gov/ccd/quickfacts.asp on November 7, 2016.

Johnson v. Joint School District No. 60, 95 Idaho 317, 508 P.2d 547 (1973).

Karp v. Becken, 477 F.2d 171, 174 (9th Cir. 1973).

Kaufman, R., & Herman, J. (1991). Strategic planning for a better society. *Educational Leadership, 48*(7), 4–8.

Kirst, M. W., & Wirt, F. M. (2009). *The political dynamics of American education* (4th ed.). Richmond, CA: McCutchan.

KOAT New Mexico. (2012, July 30). *Some schools tighten dress codes* [Video file]. Accessed at www.youtube.com/watch?v=jo3R-t_c6K4 on January 30, 2017.

Kobran, S. (2012, August 21). *Overcoming team building resistance.* Accessed at https://www.chiefoutsiders.com/blog/bid/89775/Overcoming-Team-Building-Resistance on June 3, 2017.

Kokemuller, N. (n.d.). Importance of mission vision in organizational strategy. *Houston Chronicle.* Accessed at http://smallbusiness.chron.com/importance-mission-vision-organizational-strategy-16000.html on January 30, 2017.

Kotter, J. (2008). The importance of urgency. *Harvard Business Review*. Accessed at https://hbr .org/2008/08/harvard-business-ideacast-106 on November 4, 2016.

Kouzes, J. M., & Posner, B. Z. (2003). *Credibility: How leaders gain and lose it, why people demand it.* San Francisco: Jossey-Bass.

Kundu, K., & Ganguly, D. (2014). Developing the dimensions of the effectiveness of team building in the perspective of a business organization. *ASBM Journal of Management, 7*(1), 28–43.

Lencioni, P. (2002). *The five dysfunctions of a team: A leadership fable.* San Francisco: Jossey-Bass.

Lewin, K. (1944). The dynamics of group action. *Educational Leadership, 1*(4), 195–200.

Lincoln, A. (1863). *The Gettysburg address.* Accessed at www.loc.gov/exhibits/gettysburg-address/ext /trans-nicolay-copy.html on March 31, 2017.

Lunenburg, F. C. (2010). Forces for and resistance to organizational change. *National Forum of Educational Administration and Supervision Journal, 27*(4), 1–10.

Machiavelli, N. (1950). *The prince, and the discourses.* New York: Modern Library.

Maconaquah School Corporation. (n.d.). *About us.* Accessed at www.maconaquah.k12.in.us/about_us on January 30, 2017.

Maeroff, G. I. (2011). The future of school boards. *Education Week, 30*(15), 30, 44. Accessed at www .edweek.org/ew/articles/2011/01/12/15maeroff_ep.h30.html on January 30, 2017.

Mannes, J. (2015). The problem with our school boards. *Education Week, 34*(23), 23.

Mayer, R. E. (2011). *How not to be a terrible school board member: Lessons for school administrators and board members.* Thousand Oaks, CA: Corwin Press.

McMillan, D. (n.d.). *Board bullies.* Accessed at https://www.forakergroup.org/index.php/resources /presidents-letter/board-bullies/ on June 7, 2016.

Michigan Association of School Boards (n.d.). *The importance of school board training.* Accessed at http://www.masb.org/importance-of-school-board-training.aspx on June 3, 2017.

Minichello, J. (2014, September 3). *AASA responds to Brookings Report.* Accessed at www.aasa.org /content.aspx?id=34844 on June 27, 2016.

National Center for Chronic Disease Prevention and Health Promotion. (2013). *Developing an effective evaluation report: Setting the course for effective program evaluation.* Atlanta, GA: Centers for Disease Control and Prevention. Accessed at www.cdc.gov/eval/materials/Developing-An -Effective-Evaluation-Report_TAG508.pdf on January 30, 2017.

National Center for Education Statistics. (n.d.). *Fast facts.* Accessed at https://nces.ed.gov/fastfacts /display.asp?id=28 on June 3, 2017.

National Oceanic and Atmospheric Administration. (n.d.). *NCEP wind aloft forecasts.* Accessed at http://aviationweather.gov/windtemp/data?level=l&fcst=06&region=slc&layout=on on June 26, 2017.

National School Boards Association. (n.d.). *State association services.* Accessed at www.nsba.org/services /state-association-services on November 6, 2016.

National School Boards Association. (2006). *Becoming a better board member: A guide to effective school board service* (3rd ed.). Alexandria, VA: Author.

National School Boards Association. (2016). *The key work of school boards*. Accessed at www.nsba.org /services/school-board-leadership-services/key-work on October 9, 2016.

New Albany Floyd County Consolidated School Corporation. (2010). *Minutes of board of school trustees meeting, August 23, 2010*. Accessed at https://tinyurl.com/yd5tz824 on August 27, 2017.

Olesen v. Board of Education, 676 F. Supp. 820 (N. D. Ill. 1987).

OnStrategy. (n.d.). *Phase 2: Developing strategy*. Accessed at http://onstrategyhq.com/resources /developing-your-strategy on January 30, 2017.

O'Toole, J. (1996). *Leading change: The argument for values-based leadership*. New York: Ballantine Books.

Ozimek, A. (Feb 8, 2015). The paradoxes of education reform critics. *Forbes*. Accessed at https:// www.forbes.com/sites/modeledbehavior/2015/02/08/the-paradoxes-of-education-reform-critics /#49c803ad3524 on June 3, 2017.

Park, S., Hironaka, S., Carver, P., & Nordstrum, L. (2013). *Continuous improvement in education*. Stanford, CA: Carnegie Foundation for the Advancement of Teaching.

Pollard, D. (2011, September 24). *When consensus doesn't work* [Blog post]. Accessed at http:// howtosavetheworld.ca/2011/09/24/when-consensus-doesnt-work on June 6, 2016.

Prilleltensky, I. (2000). Value-based leadership in organizations: Balancing values, interests, and power among citizens, workers, and leaders. *Ethics and Behavior, 10*(2), 139–158.

Prochaska, J. O., Norcross, J. C., & DiClemente, C. C. (1994). *Changing for good: The revolutionary program that explains the six stages of change and teaches you how to free yourself from bad habits*. New York: Morrow.

Pulliam, J. D., & Van Patten, J. J. (2003). *History of education in America* (8th ed.). Upper Saddle River, NJ: Merrill.

Rice, P. (2014). *Vanishing school boards: Where school boards have gone, why we need them, and how we can bring them back*. Lanham, MD: Rowman & Littlefield.

Rindone, N. K. (1996, May). *Effective teaming for success*. Presented at the workshop for the Kansas State Department of Education, Division of Student Support Services, Boots Adams Alumni Center, University of Kansas, Lawrence, Kansas.

Robert, H. M. (1978). *Robert's Rules of order: The classic manual of parliamentary procedure*. New York: Bell. (Original work published 1915)

Roberts, K., & Sampson, P. (2011). School board member professional development and effects on student achievement. *International Journal of Educational Management, 25*(7), pp. 701–713.

rogue. (2017). In *American heritage college dictionary*. Accessed at www.yourdictionary.com /rogue#americanheritage on November 12, 2016.

Schimmel, D., Stellman, L. R., & Fischer, L. (2014). *Teachers and the law* (9th ed.). Boston: Pearson.

Schneider, J. (Jun 22, 2016). America's not-so-broken education system. *The Atlantic*. Accessed at https://www.theatlantic.com/education/archive/2016/06/everything-in-american-education-is -broken/488189/ on June 3, 2017.

School Town of Highland. (n.d.). *School board mission, vision and core beliefs*. Accessed at www .highland.k12.in.us/administration/school_board/school_board_mission_vision_beliefs on January 30, 2017.

Scott, S. (n.d.). The 10 effective qualities of a team leader. *Houston Chronicle.* Accessed at http://smallbusiness.chron.com/10-effective-qualities-team-leader-23281.html on January 30, 2017.

Senge, P. M. (1990). *The fifth discipline: The art and practice of the learning organization.* New York: Doubleday/Currency.

Senge, P. M., & Scheetz, M. (2016, February). Systemic change and equity. In S. Petty & S. Shaffer (Eds.), *Equity-centered capacity building: Essential approaches for excellence and sustainable school system transformation* (pp. 24–33). Accessed at https://capacitybuildingnetwork.files.wordpress.com/2016/02/eccbn_volume_feb2016_final.pdf on January 30, 2017.

Sigel, I., & Saunders, R. (1977). *An inquiry into inquiry: Question-asking as an instructional model.* Washington, DC: National Institute of Education.

Smith, G. (2016, April 12). *Mission vs. vision: What's the difference?* Accessed at www.glennsmithcoaching.com/mission-vs-vision-whats-difference on January 30, 2017.

Spahr, P. (2016). *What is charismatic leadership? Leading through personal conviction.* Accessed at http://online.stu.edu/charismatic-leadership/ on August 27, 2017.

stare decisis. (2017). In *Merriam-Webster's online dictionary.* Accessed at www.merriam-webster.com/dictionary/staredecisis on September 19, 2016.

Stosich, E. L. (2014). Measuring school capacity for continuous improvement. In A. Bowers, B. Barnett, & A. Shoho (Eds.), *Using data in schools to inform leadership and decision making* (pp. 151–178). Charlotte, NC: Information Age Publishing.

Stover, D. (2010). School boards: What does the future hold? *American School Board Journal, 197*(4), 26–29.

Teacher.org. (n.d.). *How to become a superintendent.* Accessed at www.teacher.org/career/superintendent on January 30, 2017.

Tinker v. Des Moines Independent Community School District 1969 (No. 21). 393 U.S. 503 (1969). United States Supreme Court. Argued November 12, 1968. Decided February 24, 1969.

Torres, R. T., Preskill, H., & Piontek, M. E. (2005). *Evaluation strategies for communicating and reporting: Enhancing learning in organizations* (2nd ed.). Thousand Oaks, CA: Sage.

Tyack, D., & Hansot, E. (1982). *Managers of virtue: Public school leadership in America, 1820–1980.* New York: Basic Books.

Verstraete, M. (2014, March 2). *Effective questions make effective leaders* [Blog post]. Accessed at http://centerforcoachingexcellence.com/blog/2014/3/2/good-questions-make-effective-leaders on January 30, 2017.

Wagner, T. (2001). Leadership for learning: An action theory of school change. *Phi Delta Kappan, 82*(5), 378–383.

Waters, T., & Cameron, G. (2007). *The balanced leadership framework: Connecting vision with action.* Denver: Mid-continent Research for Education and Learning.

Wolf, J. R., & Bolinder, S. H. (2009). The effectiveness of home rule: A preemption and conflict analysis. *The Florida Bar Journal, 83*(6), 92.

WTAE-TV Pittsburgh. (2012, May 14). *Washington School District may change dress code* [Video file]. Accessed at www.youtube.com/watch?v=5SI-u3puwic on January 30, 2017.

[index]

The School Board Fieldbook
Mark Van Clay and Perry Soldwedel
Take a reader-friendly tour through the responsibilities and challenges of being a school board member. Award-winning administrators give practical guidance on how to best work with school administrators and staff to create and fulfill a shared vision of school system excellence.
BKF269

Leading a Learning Organization
Casey Reason
Improve the quality of organizational learning in your school. The author draws on educational, psychological, and neuroscientific research to show how leaders can change the prevailing emotional climate or tone of a school to promote deeper learning at all levels.
BKF283

Leadership 180
Dennis Sparks
This daily inspirational book contains 180 meditations for busy school leaders. Each page contains a quote focused on an essential leadership topic and a translation into a powerful "Today I will . . ." statement that integrates the reflection into daily practice.
BKF375

Shifting the Monkey
Todd Whitaker
Learn how to focus on your best employees first, and help them shift the "monkeys"—complaints, disruptions, and deflections—back to the underperformers. Through a simple and memorable metaphor, the author helps you reinvigorate your staff and transform your organization.
BKF612

Solution Tree | Press

a division of
Solution Tree

Visit SolutionTree.com or call 800.733.6786 to order.

Wait! Your professional development journey doesn't have to end with the last pages of this book.

We realize improving student learning doesn't happen overnight. And your school or district shouldn't be left to puzzle out all the details of this process alone.

No matter where you are on the journey, we're committed to helping you get to the next stage.

Take advantage of everything from **custom workshops** to **keynote presentations** and **interactive web and video conferencing**. We can even help you develop an action plan tailored to fit your specific needs.

Let's get the conversation started.

Call 888.763.9045 today.